"I love this book! It is well-organized, comprehensive, incredibly helpful, and written in a style that is easy to read and relate to. Brenda Dater's new resource is a gem for families and a must read for educators. The book offers the best and most comprehensive section I have ever read relating to sibling relationships, and includes endless tips for taking a successful family vacation. This is now one of my top five resources for parents of children on the autism spectrum."

—*Kari Dunn Buron, Autism Education Specialist and author of* When My Worries Get Too Big! *and* The Incredible 5-Point Scale

"Brenda Dater has written a real gem. I started highlighting the passages I loved, only to realize that whole pages were covered in yellow highlighter! There are so many wonderful insights and ideas in this book. One of the aspects that makes Ms. Dater's book so unique, though, is its consistent focus on parents taking care of themselves. All too often, we professionals heap on recommendation after recommendation. In our zeal to help, we may forget that parents and children are parents and children first, and individuals affected by autism second. In her own eloquent words, Ms. Dater's book reminds all of us that it is essential to heed the flight attendant's warning: 'Take care of yourself before attending to the needs of others.' I can't wait to start sharing Ms. Dater's book with the families I know."

—*Teresa Bolick, Ph.D., BCBA-D, Licensed Psychologist and Board Certified Behavior Analyst-Doctoral*

"Brenda has the rare gift of translating her parenting experience into an insightful professional guide for parents of children with ASD. It is easy to feel that she's right across the table from you having a cup of tea. Your questions get answered."

—*Elsa Abele CCC SLP, Speech/Language Pathologist and Adjunct Professor in the Center for Autism Spectrum Disorders Training, Antioch University, New England*

"It is always challenging to raise a teenager—and especially so if the person you love has Asperger's Syndrome. Brenda Dater's *Parenting without Panic* is full of helpful advice and should not only help assuage anxiety but reinforce the joy of living with somebody singular and precious."

—*Tim Page, parent, author of* Parallel Play *and Professor of Journalism and Music, University of Southern California of related interest*

**Parenting a Child with Asperger Syndrome**
**200 Tips and Strategies**
*Brenda Boyd*
ISBN 978 1 84905 941 1
eISBN 978 1 84642 420 5

**Parenting a Teen or Young Adult with Asperger**
**Syndrome (Autism Spectrum Disorder)**
**325 Ideas, Insights, Tips and Strategies**
*Brenda Boyd*
ISBN 978 1 84905 282 5
eISBN 978 0 85700 587 8

**The Complete Guide to Asperger's Syndrome**
*Tony Attwood*
ISBN 978 1 84310 495 7 (hardback)
ISBN 978 1 84310 669 2 (paperback)
eISBN 978 1 84642 559 2

**Asperger's Syndrome**
**A Guide for Parents and Professionals**
*Tony Attwood*
*Foreword by Lorna Wing*
ISBN 978 1 85302 577 8
eISBN 978 1 84642 697 1

# Parenting without Panic

A Pocket Support Group for Parents of
Children and Teens on the Autism Specrum
(Asperger's Syndrome)

Brenda Dater, MPH, MSW

Jessica Kingsley *Publishers*
London and Philadelphia

First published in 2014
by Jessica Kingsley Publishers
73 Collier Street
London N1 9BE, UK
and
400 Market Street, Suite 400
Philadelphia, PA 19106, USA

*www.jkp.com*

**Library of Congress Cataloging in Publication Data**
A CIP catalog record for this book is available from the Library of Congress

**British Library Cataloguing in Publication Data**
A CIP catalogue record for this book is available from the British Library

ISBN 978 1 84905 941 1
eISBN 978 0 85700 958 6

Printed and bound in Great Britain

To Jed, Noah, Daniel, and Josh.
Thanks for sharing our story. I'm grateful for all the
adventures we get to have as a family. I love you always.

# Contents

# Disclaimer

Stories included in this book are amalgamations of many different children and families. Some names and places have been changed to protect the privacy of minors and others discussed in this book.

# Acknowledgments

Thank you to Jessica Kingsley Publishers, and especially to Rachel Menzies, Victoria Peters, and Katelyn Bartleson, for their expert guidance, clear direction, and on-going support.

Thank you to my colleagues past and present who have helped shape my perspective on parenting. I have become a better parent and professional because of my co-workers at Portage Project in Portage, Wisconsin, Family Link in Union, New Jersey, and Asperger's Association of New England (AANE) in Watertown, Massachusetts.

Thank you to all the parents who have shared their stories and helped build a caring community.

Thank you to the supportive clinicians and educators who have helped my family thrive.

Thank you to my writing group—Jen Molinsky, Akua Sarr, and Sara Jauniskis—who saw the potential story in early drafts and encouraged me to pursue the idea.

Thank you to my valuable early readers for providing useful feedback—especially Fiona Luis, Andy Molinsky, Jim Schachter, Kathryn Collins-Wooley, Sara Jauniskis, Carolyn Thompson, Erika Drezner, Stephanie Loo, and Gail Dater.

Thank you to my extended family and friends for not taking it personally when I wasn't available and for providing sustenance in the form of walks, meals, music, and conversation.

Thank you to my children, Noah, Daniel, and Josh, for your understanding and patience as I worked on the book. Your excitement and interest were energizing! I'm so glad that I get to be your mom.

Thank you to our dog, Lavender, for making Noah smile and feel loved each and every day.

Thank you to my husband, Jed Thompson, for never faltering in your encouragement and enthusiasm for the book. Thank you for pulling double duty on the weekends so that I could write. You have shown me what it means to be a true partner and I love you. I really couldn't have done it without you.

# A Note on Terminology

While writing this book, the 2013 edition of the Diagnostic and Statistical Manual of Mental Disorders (DSM-5) was published by the American Psychiatric Association. In it, Asperger's was no longer included as a separate diagnosis, but was subsumed under the category of Autism Spectrum Disorder. Although the DSM-5 changed the diagnostic terminology, we have not yet seen a transformative shift in the diagnostic lexicon—it seems as if Asperger's is here to stay, whether it is a formal diagnosis or not.

Yet, we have to assume that some children who previously would have been given an Asperger's diagnosis will receive an autism spectrum diagnosis instead. Throughout the book, I use the terms Asperger's and autism spectrum interchangeably to address the changing diagnostic landscape. I also presume that when I refer to either Asperger's or autism spectrum, I'm including children with related conditions, such as Pervasive Developmental Disorder-Not Otherwise Specified (PDD-NOS), High Functioning Autism (HFA) and Non Verbal Learning Disorder (NVLD). Many parents whose children have these related diagnoses often find that the information and strategies for a child with Asperger's also are effective with their own child.

For ease of reading, I have used "he" or "she" instead of "s/he" in the text. The examples and strategies listed are for boys and girls regardless of which pronoun is used. When I use the word "child" or "children," I am including teenagers as well. Issues that are particularly relevant to adolescents will have headings denoting "teen," "teenager," or "adolescent."

# A Note on Strategies

Throughout the book I mention specific strategies you might try with your own child. Please do not try to implement multiple strategies simultaneously! You will get frustrated with changing too many facets of your lives all at once and so will your child. Choose one or two strategies that will address your most pressing needs at the start. Once they are familiar to you and your child, and have become a habit, you can consider trying additional approaches. Please remember that not every strategy will work for every child. Choose the ideas that seem to make the most sense for you and your family.

# CHAPTER 1

# In the Beginning

## Helicopter parents hover for a reason

I was at a meeting for professionals who work with children on the autism spectrum. We were sharing stories over lunch and the conversation veered toward the topic of "helicopter parents."

"I love the kids, but some of the parents drive me crazy," Suzanne shared.

"I know what you mean," Terry agreed. "I have a mom who emails me four times a week asking what I'm doing. I mean, I can't work with her kid if I'm always emailing her."

"Their kids are fine," added Jo. "The parents just need to relax."

So what creates the culture of panic that often accompanies parenting children with Asperger's Syndrome (AS)? Usually it's fear of the unknown. Sometimes it's guilt over the road not taken. When our children are first diagnosed, we feel a nagging pressure to have them "catch up" with their peers. Transitions or lifecycle events bring the developmental chasm between our children and their peers to the forefront. Frustration can turn into panic when we feel as if our children's helpers aren't helping. We are bombarded with conflicting messages telling us how to help our children succeed. We try to comprehend and predict what they need, but panic fills in for doubt as we wonder if we are right. We need to delve beneath the "helicopter parent" label and uncover the root of the problem—fear over the uncertain future our children face.

## Redefining normal

Panic comes from the belief that typical development is normal and atypical (unpredictable) development is abnormal. It comes from feeling like a minority when the world around you expects and celebrates being typical. But atypical development is typical for us—it is our *new* normal. We have to forge a fresh path where parents and children believe it is okay to be different and celebrate the unique perspective our children offer. Accepting our children for who they are does not mean that parenting them is easy or that we won't help them learn new skills or understand concepts that don't come naturally to them. We can let go of "catch-up-itis" *and* encourage their social and emotional growth.

Hovering over our children isn't helpful, but it makes sense. Panic increases when we feel our concerns aren't taken seriously and our children are misunderstood or mistreated. So how do we stop ourselves from panicking endlessly? We'll feel less frenzied when we don't expect our children to duplicate the developmental path of typical peers. We'll panic less when we find a community of parents who understand what daily life is like for our family. And as we find effective approaches and strategies, we'll feel more capable of handling the challenges that come our way.

Let's get started.

## The parent–professional combination

When people find out that I'm a professional who works at Asperger's Association of New England (AANE) and I have a child with Asperger's, they often ask, "Did you work in special needs before your children were born or did you get into the field after you knew your child had a diagnosis?"

"The work came first," I reply.

"You're so lucky you have that knowledge. It must make being a parent of a child on the spectrum easier."

I know what people mean, but I'm not sure that there are any shortcuts to feeling confident and capable when parenting a child with AS. I agree that my understanding of Asperger's and Attention Deficit Hyperactivity Disorder (ADHD) has been beneficial. At the same time, the challenges my children face feel just as raw and unsettling as they do to any other parent. I get that hollowed-out feeling in the pit of my stomach when my child is excluded. I don't always have the energy to do the pre-planning that's often required before participating in a new event or activity. I have gotten overwhelmed and worried about school meetings. Some weeks, months, and years have kept me on high alert, and I've had to learn how to stay calm and cope with long-term challenges. Not that any of these stressors has made me love my children less.

As a parent of children with special needs, I know what it's like to have school papers covering every flat surface in the house, a sick child and pet needing attention, and a play date gone wrong. I know how frustrating it can be to have children who always need to have the last word in any discussion. I have also felt exhausted by the amount of effort it takes to get everyone out of the house in the morning and tucked back in for a decent night's sleep at the end of the day. None of these responsibilities is easy. As parents, we need practical ideas that take our day-to-day reality into account and help set expectations that can be achieved.

## Connecting to AANE

I felt as if I'd hit the jackpot when I found AANE. My husband and I were contemplating a move to Massachusetts from New Jersey. We had three young children, all with special needs. I couldn't fathom starting over in a new place unless I knew there was support and understanding of Asperger's. I did what many parents do after their children are asleep for the night; I turned to the internet to research resources in our prospective new community. I found AANE on my first attempt and was completely captivated. They answered my questions and shared information. They gave me names of parents in the towns we were considering moving into. They directed me to local resources. I remember telling my husband, "We have to move to Watertown" so that we could be near AANE.

The Association was my lifeline during the tremendously stressful mid-school-year move. I was able to connect with other parents and professionals. With all that was new in our lives, AANE grounded me. Little did I know that a year after our move, I would be in a position to join the staff. My work provided the opportunity to blend my professional and parenting expertise. Through phone calls, emails, support groups, and workshops it became clear that parents were raising the same types of concerns and questions repeatedly. We wanted to provide a way for families to connect and support each other while having their concerns addressed and validated. And so "parent topic nights" were born—to help parents find practical information, support, and community.

## AANE parent topic nights

Topic nights cover the concerns that parents voice most frequently. Parents often feel anxious as they speculate about their child's opportunities to make friends. They wonder how to talk with their child about his diagnosis. They feel completely overwhelmed by the less structured and more open-ended time on holidays and vacations. Parents are startled by how their children interact and wonder how to meet the needs of multiple children living under the same roof. At topic nights, we begin by taking the pulse of the group to hear about the most pressing concerns. Once we have a better sense of the specific questions and trepidations surrounding any given topic, we explain why the challenges exist and offer practical strategies. Topic nights provide an evening of information, conversation, and connection. Parents leave feeling understood, validated, and better informed.

Parenting is never an easy job, but it is made easier by connecting with others. For parents who have a child with Asperger's, or a related diagnosis, that means connecting to other parents who implicitly understand your daily life. Parents' shoulders relax and their foreheads stop creasing as they realize they are not the only family to struggle with a particular issue. I wrote this book as a way to extend that sense of relief for families who can't attend topic nights.

Throughout the chapters, I will move between examples and conversations from previous parent topic nights and experiences in my own family. The family stories reflect amalgamations from the hundreds of families with whom I have worked. As you read the conversations, imagine that you've been transported into the room with 40 other parents and are listening in as they share their concerns, frustrations, and ideas. You are no longer alone with your worries. You have found a community that understands what it's like to live with Asperger's.

But before I introduce you to other families, you should get to know mine.

## The A word

Like all families, we have our story—the day when our hypotheses were confirmed that our child was different from the majority. Blocks, books, and babies surrounded us as we waited for our son's developmental checkup. My 3-year-old sat quietly, reading his book about trucks, as my husband and I sat in silence.

"We can see Noah now in room number four," the nurse called out to us. Jed and I stood quickly and began walking to the door, with Noah reluctantly walking in between us, his eyes still on his book.

Noah began speaking with the doctor as soon as she entered the room.

"I saw an articulated truck on the highway…"

"He has Asperger's," the doctor quickly told us. I had suspected as much from my work in early intervention and comments and discussions with colleagues, but I still couldn't get over how quickly she came to the determination. She hadn't been in the room with him for more than 90 seconds.

"How can you say that?" I asked. "How can you know for certain?"

"His prosody," she replied quickly. "His tone of voice and the way he speaks are a dead giveaway."

"What about all the characteristics of Asperger's he doesn't have?" I asked. "How many characteristics or traits does he need to be diagnosed?"

"Well, maybe he doesn't have Asperger's," the doctor responded. "We could send him to a speech pathologist for the prosody."

"No, I'm not saying he doesn't have it," I explained. "I'm asking how and when you know with confidence that a child has Asperger's?"

"Let's get an appointment with a neurologist and developmental pediatrician," the doctor suggested.

And so it began. Our shift from a family with a 3-year-old who loved all things truck, would spend hours looking at books, and had developmental delays in fine and gross motor skills, to a child with a diagnosis of Asperger's confirmed by a developmental pediatrician and neurologist. What we couldn't fathom at the time was that this was *not* a temporary glitch we would be able to "fix" through some kind of short-term treatment. Part of our confusion was due to diagnosticians and clinicians telling us that he was "high functioning" and had "mild" Asperger's, implying that he would catch up with his peers. I don't find these qualifiers helpful as a professional or use them when describing my own children. Maybe other professionals use them as a way to offer a hopeful message when children are first diagnosed. As a parent, I'm not sure it was comforting. It led to our disillusionment and unrealistic expectations regarding how quickly Noah would overcome his challenges. When Noah's progress didn't match professional assertions we felt like failures—and assumed there was something wrong with us. The reality was that Noah's atypical development would not follow the predictable course of his peers.

When you're the parent of a newly diagnosed child, you feel raw, as if you live with your nerve endings continuously exposed. I don't feel that way most of the time anymore. But certain situations still elicit a visceral response. Through the years we have had caring and skilled professionals working alongside us in and outside of the various schools our children attended. Unfortunately, there were also professionals who caused emotional upheaval by miscalculating Noah's needs or abilities or making pronouncements regarding his future. Although the professional side of me knew to ask questions and advocate for what Noah needed, the parent in me wanted thoughtful discussion and guidance through the inherent uncertainty that parenting children with special needs brings.

## Parent partners

We were looking for a partner in the process who could see the big picture. When we met with professionals, they would look at Noah through the lens of their own discipline and make recommendations from their perspective. But rarely could they show us how to combine all the different recommendations to provide a practical and coordinated approach. We were left to figure out which area of need was greatest and how we could divide our time, money, and energy to address each one in turn. We yearned for someone to take all the information, put it in a blender, press liquefy, and come up with a plan that had the correct amount of each therapeutic ingredient to make an effective intervention smoothie.

Ferreting out which need was greatest and how we could best support Noah's learning was challenging. We realized early on that there wasn't a professional whose job it was to be the general contractor; that job was reserved for us. We had to integrate the information and determine what questions needed to be asked and answered. We learned this lesson the hard way after hoping and expecting someone else to take charge and direct us. It was not unlike the feelings we had when we took Noah home from the hospital as a newborn. As we strapped him in the car seat and got ready to drive away, Jed and I looked at each other skeptically and said, "Are they really letting us take him home? By ourselves? That doesn't seem like a very good idea." But just as we grew into Noah's parents and didn't have those same anxieties when we brought our second son home from the hospital, we grew into parenting a child with Asperger's and gained comfort in our new role with time, support, information, and patience.

## Feeling vulnerable and looking for answers

Like all parents faced with new information, we were concerned about what this meant for our son's future. Would he ever have friends? Would he be able to go to a regular school? What was the best way for us to help him? How would we explain this to our families and friends? How could we make sure he grew up knowing he was valued and that we didn't think a diagnosis made him "less than?" We knew that Noah was the same boy the day after his diagnosis as he was the day before. But this new information catapulted us firmly into the special needs parenting camp. No longer would Noah catch up to his peers' development; he would be on his own uneven and unpredictable path.

Parents of young, newly diagnosed children, or children and teens going through major life transitions, are vulnerable to the expert opinion bias of professionals. Parents are looking to professionals to guide them in their decision-making. No parent wants to make a major misstep and set his or her child back or miss an opportunity that could be life changing. Professionals have tremendous power at this stage as parents begin to digest what Asperger's means to their child and family. We, like many other families, sought out discussion with the professionals working with our son. Often, when we asked questions, professionals seemed resolute about what Noah needed. We felt less sure and weren't looking for certainty, as appealing and hope-affirming as that would have been, but rather, honest and open discussion about the pros and cons of various educational and therapeutic approaches we might try.

Near the end of the pre-school year I approached Noah's teacher to ask about which classroom might be a good fit for him in the next year.

"I don't know why you'd want to change, he's got a lot of needs," she answered, turning toward the door.

"I'd like to consider the integrated classroom at the school," I explained. The class Noah was currently in was segregated; only children who had been classified as needing special education were enrolled. The class I was interested in included children with and without disabilities. It seemed like a model that might work well for my son.

"He'll never be able to manage," the teacher reiterated. "That classroom doesn't have enough support. He needs to stay in our program. You'd be making a mistake."

I didn't agree with his teacher's assessment and was surprised by her negative reaction. I felt abandoned and uncertain about how to navigate and discover which setting would be the right fit. But being a professional helped me know which questions to ask and which people to include in meetings when decisions needed to be made. Instead of taking his teacher's comments as the only valid perspective, I brought this question to the larger team to talk about what supports Noah would need in order to be part of the inclusive classroom. It's important to recognize that there is rarely only one way to provide an appropriate program. We need to consider all educational options; not only the ones already tried or familiar.

Our confusion with finding the right educational program continued. When it was time for Noah to transition to middle school, there were a few options available and multiple meetings with professionals from all the programs. We were losing sleep over the decision and sought out discussion to try and clarify the right choice for Noah.

"Why should we consider program 'x'?" we asked.

"He'll never be able to manage at program 'y,'" we were told by multiple people.

"But program 'y' is where his friends are going," we explained. "Shouldn't we keep him with his friends?"

"Middle school children change friendships anyway," another teacher clarified. "He probably won't keep any of the same friends, so I wouldn't worry about it."

"But if he goes to program 'x' he won't be with anyone he knows and we don't know any of the parents there," we continued. "We can't help him connect to kids in the school through their families. We think he'll be miserable without the familiarity of the friends he's made."

"I really wouldn't worry about it," we were told. "Program 'x' will provide all the social instruction he needs. Program 'y' will be a lot more work for you."

"We don't mind working hard to get the right program in place," we continued. "But we can't make new friends for him. Couldn't you consult with program 'y' so that he can remain with his friends *and* get the services he needs?" we asked.

A prolonged silence fell upon the table. Finally a school professional responded.

"Sending your son to our program will give him the best chance for learning what he needs to learn," she said. "You shouldn't base your decision on the friends he has now because that will probably change and he may end up with no friends and a program that's insufficient if you go to program 'y.'"

## Putting professional recommendations into context

I wondered why these educational professionals were certain that my son's wish to stay with his friends was less important than the program components. What he needed was both: access to the social capital generated by his friendships, which is no small accomplishment for a child with Asperger's, *and* a program that provided all the specialized instruction he needed. But if he couldn't have both, I would prioritize friends over program. I knew I could work with the school to develop a program but I wouldn't be able to build a community of friends when I knew no one at the new school and I wouldn't be there to help make connections. I grappled with this decision because the professionals at "x" seemed committed and the program looked terrific on paper. But my gut told me that keeping the tie to friends was more important and harder to recreate; and so we went with program "y." Six years later I can say it was the right choice.

Professional judgments promising unrealistic results or predicting disaster make me wary. Whenever I have been on the receiving end of this type of information I have felt pressure to do what is recommended even if my instinct pulls me in a different direction. I'm searching for knowledgeable professionals who have the ability to see beyond their own specialized lens and consider what my child needs in an objective manner. We need to remember that our parental wisdom matters. Our gut reactions and instincts concerning our child need to be considered alongside professional recommendations.

## Introducing Daniel: The double A

As a parent, concerns arise constantly, whether you have the energy for them or not. We would soon learn that our second son needed more from us than we had been anticipating.

Our middle son, Daniel, followed his older brother's social emotional trajectory in pre-school. Daniel wasn't easily soothed. He was always in motion. He had a hard time sleeping. Little changes in his daily routine would set him off on a crying jag. He had an infectious smile. When he was content, playing with Lego or Play-Doh, he looked serene. Due to his older brother's diagnosis, and his own challenges with self-regulation, Daniel easily qualified for early intervention and the integrated pre-school program in our town. As he moved into kindergarten, and went through neuropsychological evaluations, he was given the diagnosis of ADHD and Asperger's.

On the day Daniel received his diagnosis I was standing in front of the school talking with a friend when Daniel was reprimanded by another parent.

"Stop that!" she yelled at Daniel as he was trying to play with her child. Daniel was forever getting in other children's personal space. He didn't recognize that other people might need an inch or two between his body and theirs. Daniel looked at me with his beautiful blue eyes as tears started to form. I wish I could say I just walked away from the other parent. But I was feeling raw and empty. I wanted to protect Daniel from all the people who had already made him feel bad about himself and all the people who would do so in the future. I knew this was an impossible task, but all I could think was, he's had enough, let him be. "Leave him alone," I responded in a trembling voice. "If you have a problem with my kid, talk to me, not him. He's had a hard day."

I was greeted with an icy stare as this mom walked away in a hurry. It wasn't a controlled response, but I felt that it was all I could manage in my sensitized state. I was steeling myself for the years ahead when I would have to explain and apologize for the social mistakes Daniel would make unintentionally and with great regret. Daniel wanted to do the right thing and would think he was a terrible person when he made an innocent mistake. I wish the parent who reprimanded him could've seen that side of him and been helpful instead of harmful.

We knew that Daniel was the same lovable boy—the diagnoses hadn't changed him. As I sat in the meeting reviewing the evaluation report, I felt like my world was closing in on me. How was I ever going to be able to meet the needs of two kids with special needs? I had become an Asperger's expert because of Noah—but how would I have the time to become an expert for Daniel? I felt overwhelmed and depressed. I felt as if I wasn't up to the challenge. I felt completely helpless.

For the first five years of Noah's life, I had been able to focus on him exclusively, and yet I hadn't been able to give Daniel that same level of attention and support during his first five years. At times I had felt exasperated with Daniel when he needed me because Noah also needed me on a 24/7 basis. Part of me felt as if Daniel wasn't allowed to have any special needs because my energy was tapped out and I wasn't sure how I would find more. I never felt as if there was enough of me to go around and it seemed that I was shortchanging one child or another. When the boys were both young, I often felt as if I couldn't possibly meet all their needs. All I wanted to do was love and enjoy them, but I frequently felt frustrated and overwhelmed by the amount of structure and support they both needed in order to make sense of the world around them and feel safe venturing into it.

Just as I tell other parents after their child is diagnosed, "You won't feel this way forever," my initial emotions evolved— allowing me to become more proactive and supportive. Our understanding of Daniel's diagnosis changed through the years too. We knew Daniel had many traits of Asperger's, but his needs and strengths were different from Noah's. Daniel was acutely tuned in to others' emotional states and would soak up their stress and anxiety. We recognized that the interventions Noah needed were not the same approaches we'd recommend for Daniel. When Daniel's latest evaluations confirmed the ADHD diagnosis, we weren't surprised. Although the evaluator acknowledged his Asperger-like traits—especially anxiety— Daniel was close, but did not surpass, the threshold for diagnosis. Like many parents, we have a child who doesn't fit neatly into a diagnosis, but still needs our understanding and acceptance of how he experiences the world around him.

## Coping with chaos

My professional background proved a benefit to managing the divergent needs of our growing boys. Throughout the years, we had visual schedules, calendars, and chore charts. We previewed and cued and facilitated and monitored and processed. We reached out to other families and hosted play dates. We ran a summer program in our home around the special interests of our children. We started hiking clubs, game nights, and book groups. We did a tour of playgrounds in the area to practice playing with kids we didn't know. We cuddled and read books and took swim lessons. We went to therapy and school and tried to add new foods to diets. We did all these things and wondered if we should do more or less.

We were on alert. We anticipated what our kids might need to be explained to them and which situations might be challenging. We acted as interpreters for them—explaining the larger world to them, building their understanding and skills for managing and interacting with others, and translating their confusing behaviors to people so they wouldn't be misunderstood. At times it was exhausting. Often it was a good balance of working on challenges and enjoying interests. We tried not to do too many interventions at once as we would all be overwhelmed, but to recognize when we might need to shift our focus.

## And then came Josh

When Daniel was in pre-school, Josh was born. He didn't talk until he was almost 3. Josh kept up the family tradition of being eligible for early intervention and special education, with speech and occupational therapy as his main supports. Josh had a warm and loving pre-school teacher who helped us handle the challenges of parenting three young children with special needs. She saw all the potential in Josh and helped him find his voice. By the time he left pre-school, he had become a leader in his class and enjoyed playing with other kids. Josh was never on the autism spectrum.

## Lifelong parenting

As of this writing, I am in the transition to college for my oldest son. It feels reminiscent of the early years. There is no shortage of professional advice offering opinions on what we should do— gap year, fifth year of high school, straight to residential college, a four-year college and live at home, or start at community college and then transfer. It's wonderful and terrifying that the options are endless. There is no precise clear path for my son, or most kids with Asperger's, and no one can tell us with certainty which intervention, program, or school will be the right fit. I know that the way through this very uncertain time is to assess my son's needs and interests, learn about the options available, and try to find a match between the two. Through my work I've seen many bright Asperger's college students fail because of the social, self-advocacy, and executive functioning demands required in a college environment. None of our children will be "fully formed" when they leave high school; we are trying to set the stage for continued growth and learning through experiences that offer just the right amount of challenge.

## Lessons learned

Understanding Asperger's and how it affects my child has helped me ask the right questions of professionals and search out or develop the activities, programs, and school approaches that will help him build the skills he needs to be out in the world and connect to others. Being a professional has not protected me from the emotional extremes, anxious moments, burnout, or frustration. It also doesn't lessen the intense joy I feel when my children reach challenging milestones, like riding a bike, sleeping through the night, running, having a friend, or being able to try new experiences. As parents, we can feel overwhelmed by professional recommendations. But my professional expertise has helped me recognize when more information or caution is necessary.

## What my professional experience has taught me as a parent

- *Ask questions*: Whether it is a school program, course of treatment, or intervention, ask how the proposed course of action fits your child's needs and what data or experience support the professional recommendations.

- *Seek out information*: Staying up to date on the laws/ regulations affecting children on the spectrum and having practical examples of how others are addressing their children's needs has been helpful when I'm working with professionals on behalf of my own children.

- *Connect to other parents*: I work with other parents and professionals who have children with AS. It is helpful to have a peer group that understands your worries and celebrates your child's successes (even when they aren't the typical ones).

- *Expect glitches*: Even when you have a good plan in place, unexpected problems will arise—that's just part of life. When glitches occur, try to put them in perspective and consider what you, your child, and the professionals who work with you can learn from the experience. You don't have to like it—but you will recover more quickly when you understand that occasional bumps in the road are inevitable.

## Setting panic aside

Isolation increases our sense of fear, anxiety, or depression as we wonder whether we are doing the right thing for our children. Throughout the chapters, you will see that many other parents share your concerns. Each chapter will bring explanations, examples, stories, and practical strategies to help you feel more confident about how to address daily parenting dilemmas.

There is a big community of parents out there, facing tough challenges like the ones you face. I hope that this book helps you feel connected, eases your stress, and offers you the information you need to parent without panic.

CHAPTER 2 ——————————————————————

# Behavior

*Looking Through an Asperger's Lens*

What words come to mind when you think about your child's behavior? Do you ever think he is disrespectful, lazy, arrogant, rude, or unwilling? Many parents feel the same way. When we describe our child's behavior in these terms, it leads us to think that he is being difficult on purpose, which in turn leads us to respond punitively. Yet our discipline doesn't seem to make the challenging behavior diminish.

The developmental stage our children are experiencing *and* Asperger's impact their behavior. There is a plethora of advice for parents of typical kids on how to address the expected challenges of any developmental phase. When we try to apply this advice without considering how Asperger's fits in the behavioral picture, we are all likely to become annoyed.

We've all been there—we have some tools and approaches that may work with one child, but completely backfire with another. Or it worked when the kids were younger, but now those same approaches are entirely ineffective. Perhaps other parents or family members keep telling us that if we just were more consistent with these tried and true approaches that worked for their kids, we'd have calm, flexible kids of our own.

Let's be clear that no parent is perfect. No strategy, tool, or approach is perfect. No child is perfect. So we should not expect perfection from our approaches, our kids, or ourselves. We need to cut each other some slack and not beat ourselves up when we have one of those days when nothing seems to work, everyone's on edge, and we wish we could go to bed, pull the covers up, and call it a day.

The frustration parents and kids often feel about behavior boils down to expectations, and assumptions about what causes "inappropriate" or "unexpected" behavior. When you repeatedly witness a behavior that is different from what you expected, it's easy to allow the behavior to trigger a visceral response. If you believe your child is doing something socially unacceptable *intentionally*, it's hard to stay calm, step back, and take time to think about trying different strategies. But if you understand that her behavior is likely the result of her lack of knowledge, lack of awareness of the situation, or inability to apply a skill she knows, then it is easier to respond with compassion when your child shows a behavior you wish she wouldn't.

I've heard Asperger's described as "social dyslexia" (Howlin 2003). Just as someone who has dyslexia has trouble deciphering written language, someone with Asperger's struggles to comprehend verbal and nonverbal *social* language. How we communicate socially is so confusing! Words have different meanings depending on their context. We vary our tone of voice, volume, and facial expressions to make our message clear without clearly stating verbally what our message is. Our conversations and requests don't follow linear, logical thinking much of the time. We assume understanding, when there might be none. We infer meaning, when the intention may have been quite different. Just as someone with dyslexia needs a specialized approach to understand written language, someone with social dyslexia requires explicit teaching and facilitated practice in the social curriculum.

It is a challenge for a neurotypical person—someone who is not on the autism spectrum—to understand why and how someone with AS continually makes social mistakes. Neurotypical people tend to process social information quickly, efficiently, and intuitively. They don't know *how* they know what they are supposed to do in different types of social situations. They don't know *how* they learned it. They just know.

In his book, *Autism As Context Blindness*, Dr. Peter Vermeulen explains that one of the main difficulties in autism is the lack of spontaneous use of context (Vermeulen 2012). Children with Asperger's don't automatically decipher the important social cues that would clarify how to respond in different situations. That's why they make social mistakes and seem perplexed by the reaction of those around them. Their behavior appears "inappropriate" or "unexpected" because it doesn't match the setting they are in. If they were tuned in to the subtle social rules inherent in the various situations they face, their out-of-sync behavior would most likely decrease.

Many parents feel conflicted about the cause of their child's behavioral challenges. They wonder if they are letting their child, "off the hook," if they don't respond with a strong consequence or punishment. Yet, they might sense that in order to change how their child behaves, they may need to alter their long-held beliefs about what's causing the problems and how to respond to them. This chapter will help you understand *why* it's challenging for our children to display social competence. You'll learn about the factors that are impacting or influencing their behavior. And you'll see how to interpret their challenging behavior through an Asperger's lens. Practical, specific strategies will be embedded in Chapters 3 to 10 to illustrate how you can more effectively respond when challenges arise.

Throughout this chapter on behavior, you will learn that:

- showing socially competent behavior requires complex skills, as can be seen by examining:
  - Asperger's Syndrome / autism spectrum: the big picture
  - why our children struggle with behavior
- behavior can be interpreted differently:
  - reconsidering "difficult" behavior
  - looking through an Asperger's lens.

## Asperger's Syndrome: the big picture

Parents' concerns often focus on their child's inability to demonstrate social competence consistently—taking each unique social context into account and responding as others would expect. Our children have to expend greater effort to try to understand and respond to the complex social situations they encounter. Figure 2.1 (Dater 2008) conveys the array of factors that impact our children's ability to show socially competent behavior regularly. Because our children struggle to learn and apply these skills, they require explicit teaching and coaching to highlight the important information that others learn implicitly.

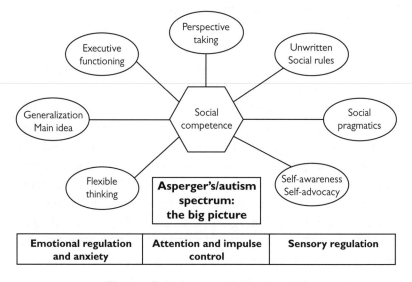

**Figure 2.1**: Asperger's Syndrome/
autism spectrum: the big picture

Let's consider why our children have difficulties in these areas and how we can interpret "difficult" behavior differently when we assess it through an Asperger's lens.

## Consider emotional regulation

My son came home from his summer program with a quiet voice. I had been out walking the dog and came across him walking home from the bus.

"Hey Mom, did camp call you yet?" he asked.

"No," I answered, my breath rate increasing as I wondered why camp needed to call.

"Well, I got punched today," Noah said as he bent down to pet the dog. "Not a good day."

"I'm sorry that happened," I said. "What was going on when you got punched?"

"We were playing a board game and everyone at the table had agreed on the rules except this one kid," Noah explained. "He kept saying that we needed to play different rules and he wouldn't give up. I kept telling him to shut up and he wouldn't. So finally I called him a 'jackass' and he punched me in the arm."

Like many children with AS, Noah has struggled to understand and manage the strong emotions he feels. When frustrated, confused, annoyed, anxious, or stressed, our children may seem to overreact to the situation. What parents and professionals might not realize is that they truly feel that the situation is dire and needs to change immediately to relieve intense feelings, sensations, or thoughts. It is very difficult for our children to respond calmly when they feel under attack.

*Interpreting behavior through an Asperger's lens*

THE DEMANDS OF THE SITUATION SURPASSED
MY CHILD'S CURRENT CAPABILITIES

"Oh Noah," I sighed as I looked at the ground. I thought we were past this stage of losing his temper. I thought he had enough strategies to handle rising frustrations. But, new situation, new people, less structure, and now we see the behavior again.

"Look, I already got a lecture at camp," Noah said. "I know I shouldn't have sworn or told him to shut up. I know I should've walked away. I kept thinking he would just be quiet at some point, but he didn't stop. It's his fault I lost my temper."

"No Noah, it's never someone else's fault when we lose our tempers," I said. "Only we have control over what we do with the strong emotions we feel. I can certainly understand why that situation was frustrating for you. I understand that in that moment you didn't see or feel like you had any other choice and so you swore. But that's why it's so important to think about what you'll do before you get really frustrated. What helps you calm down when situations bother you?"

"I already talked about this at camp," Noah answered. "I'm going to listen to music when I feel irritated. Music always calms me down."

"That's one idea," I replied. "What about taking a break and walking away if you're in a situation that's starting to get out of control?"

"Got it, got it," Noah said quickly. "Take a break. Can we please stop talking about this now? I don't need another lecture and I already feel bad enough. Why can't I ever express how I feel? I'm angry and I need to get it out. Just leave me alone."

"I understand your request," I said. "Could you please try saying that again without the angry tone?"

"Will you please leave me alone?" Noah asked in a neutral tone.

"Okay we'll revisit this once I talk with camp," I replied. "But for now, let's find something to do that helps you feel calm. I'm sorry you had a hard day."

It's important to remember that our children are doing the best they can with the skills they have in any given moment. When they have meltdowns we need to stay calm so that we can help them regain their composure. Only then can we help them think through possible triggers and potential solutions.

### Consider anxiety

In his book, *The Complete Guide to Asperger's Syndrome*, Tony Attwood states that, "We all feel a little anxious sometimes, but many children and adults with Asperger's Syndrome appear to be prone to being anxious for much of their day, or to be extremely anxious about a specific event" (Attwood 2007, p.136). When we're anxious we become less flexible in our thinking and problem solving. Often our children use the only strategies they know—meltdowns, rigid thinking, or avoidance—as a response to anxiety-producing situations (Attwood 2007).

I know that when I'm feeling anxious about something, my social skills aren't as sharp and it's hard for me to pay attention to others' needs. If I felt anxious all the time it would be harder to appear socially competent. Our kids struggle to stay calm and cope with situations, people, and activities that frustrate them. Even when we teach our children strategies, their anxiety may make it hard for them to use the skills they've learned.

At our recent topic night on behavior, Suzanne, mom to 8-year-old Connor, was concerned about Connor's teacher.

"His teacher keeps telling me that Connor is out of control," Suzanne explained. "Here's what we talked about yesterday."

"Connor had a hard day today," his teacher told Suzanne after school. "He didn't want to go to music and threw a tantrum."

Suzanne felt her heart beating faster and asked, "What was happening before music?"

"I was reading a story to the class and I had to cut it short because our music time was moved up," his teacher explained. "I asked everyone to line up, but Connor didn't follow my directions and started yelling at me and ripping the papers on his desk."

"I'm sure the change in schedule made him feel anxious." Suzanne said.

"I don't think so," his teacher replied. "He didn't look anxious to me."

## Interpreting behavior through an Asperger's lens
I NEED TO INVESTIGATE IF MY CHILD'S ANXIETY
IS CONTRIBUTING TO HER MELTDOWNS

Anxiety can manifest in many forms. It's important to learn how your child shows her anxiety. Some children will be able to say they feel stressed or anxious and pinpoint the source of their anxiety. Others will feel anxious, but may not be able to identify the feeling or situations that make it increase. Don't assume your child isn't anxious because she doesn't show classic signs. Your child might show her anxiety by doing any of the following:

- asking questions repeatedly

- pacing

- increasing voice volume

- running away

- hitting

- grimacing

- turning red

- clenching fists

- making negative comments

- tearing paper

- throwing things

- swearing

- eating continuously.

It's also important to consider which environments make your child feel comfortable. When my son is at ease with others, he makes eye contact, asks questions, listens, and seems relaxed. When he is feeling anxious he's likely to pace and ask to leave. The environment our children are in impacts which skills they are able to use and how anxious they feel.

## Consider attention and impulse control

At a recent parent topic night on behavior, Claire, the parent of a 9-year-old, talked about how she couldn't get Christopher off his computer and wasn't sure what to do.

"Christopher loves being on screens all day long. I've tried limiting it or taking it away, but then he throws such a fit, we can't function. He's so happy and calm while he's connected to electronics; I'm glad he has something that he enjoys because much of his day stresses him. But it is hard to get him to do his homework and chores and it's a huge fight to go to sleep. Some friends tell me I should take it away completely. Others tell me I should let him have it because it's his 'special interest.' All I know is that I'm getting so frustrated and I'm afraid I'm going to say or do something I'll regret."

Claire is right that taking away a special interest as a consequence or punishment is not a good idea. It's one of the few ways Christopher relieves the deep anxiety he feels. At the same time, expanding the ways in which Christopher can feel calmer is worth focusing on so that we avoid his singular dependence on screens to soothe frustrations or intense feelings (Attwood 2007).

### Interpreting behavior through an Asperger's lens

MY CHILD ISN'T CAPABLE OF CONTROLLING HIS
IMPULSIVE BEHAVIOR INDEPENDENTLY, YET

Remember when your child was a toddler and you locked up all the cleaning supplies and medicines so that he didn't accidently ingest them? We would never have dreamt of leaving poisonous substances out in plain sight—we assumed that our children needed us to set safety limits. Our impulsive children also need limits. They don't yet have the internal barometer that tells them to stop and think before acting. So if we leave highly desirable items in their reach, they will seek them out. Expecting impulsive kids to be able to stop themselves without help is unrealistic.

## Consider sensory regulation

Many of our children don't feel comfortable in their own skin. They either appear overly sensitive to certain types of sensory input, actively avoiding it, *or* crave it and seek it out. Sensory sensitivities to sound, lights, touch, smell, movement, or taste can make them appear "difficult."

It took my son a long time to learn to swim. We had to break down each step, go slowly, and practice numerous times before he felt comfortable swimming. A couple of years after he learned, he attended a summer camp that required him to jump off the dock in order to pass the deep-water test.

"I'm not jumping off the dock," Noah fumed.

"Noah, if you want to be able to take boats out, you have to take the deep water test," I explained. "The test includes jumping off the dock. What bothers you about it?"

"I hate having both my feet leave the ground at the same time," he replied. "It makes me uncomfortable."

"What if we practice doing it slowly at the pool?" I asked. "You could slide in first and then you could hop in while still having one foot on the ground."

"No," he yelled. "I can't do it. Why do we need to be able to jump in anyway? It's stupid."

"My guess is that they want to be sure if you fell in deep water accidentally, you would be okay," I answered. "I know it makes you uncomfortable to have both feet off the ground at once, but whenever we've gone slowly and practiced, you've been able to manage. We can help you with this and they could help you at camp too. What do you think?"

"No way," he said. "I'm not doing it."

Noah was not being difficult on purpose. His body experiences sensations intensely. Jumping off the dock feels like bungee jumping to him. Our bodies can process sensory information quite differently, which can make using our bodies to accomplish complex motor tasks (like bike riding, writing, tying shoelaces, throwing or catching a ball, or walking in a crowded space without bumping into others) challenging.

*Interpreting behavior through an Asperger's lens*

I NEED TO BE AWARE OF THE SENSORY

STRESSES MY CHILD IS EXPERIENCING

Recently my three boys did a photo shoot with our dog. I didn't think it would be hard for them because they love holding the dog and they knew it would support AANE. But then my fantasy bumped up against reality.

"Mom I can't kneel on the ground," Noah said. "I don't like any part of my body touching the ground except my feet."

"Noah, I think you can do it," I replied. "How about just kneeling and holding onto the bench?"

"No," he responded. "I can't do it."

"Okay, how about lying down on the grass instead?" I asked.

"Mom, that's still putting other parts of my body on the ground," Noah clarified. "What part of, 'I don't like any part of my body touching the ground except my feet' did you not understand?"

"Okay Noah," I said. "I know it feels uncomfortable to you. But I also know that sometimes when you try something you think you won't be able to tolerate, you can. How about you try it and if it's too much, you can stand right back up?"

"I'll try it," Noah answered. "But how many more poses do we have to do? It makes me uncomfortable to have people touching me. I feel claustrophobic."

"You seem okay with touching the dog," I said. "Think of your brothers as larger dogs without much fur."

"Good one," Noah said. "Seriously, how much longer?"

"I know it's hard for you," I said. "We can add in more breaks and think of poses that don't require your brothers to touch you too much. Why don't you just play with the dog for a little while and then we'll do a few more."

I didn't say what first came to mind, which was, "Stop complaining. You'll be fine. Just kneel down and look at the photographer." If I'd said what I was thinking, I would've been dismissing Noah's experience and encouraging his anxiety to increase. I don't honestly know if he could've done the poses he said he couldn't, but in that moment I wasn't going to convince him otherwise by pushing. I needed to acknowledge his sensory sensitivities and offer him ways to relax or work around them.

## Consider flexibility

Our kids can come across as stubborn. They don't easily shift from one activity to another. They have difficulty agreeing to activities that either don't appeal to them or appear challenging. Sometimes our children can seem completely unreasonable when they reject our requests. But they most likely have their own agenda and haven't considered that ours might differ. Asking them to change their plan increases their anxiety—leading to less flexibility.

At a recent parent topic night, Jason, dad of 8-year-old Jerome, wondered why his son was so "difficult."

"We were at a work sponsored picnic. Some of the boys were playing Magic the Gathering and Jerome joined in. It's one of his special interests and he knows all the arcane rules. The other kids were having fun with the game, but they weren't following *all* the rules. Jerome kept telling them that they were wrong and demanding they change how they were playing the game. He couldn't let it go and finally the boys got tired of him and left. Jerome got really mad at the boys for leaving, but didn't see the part he played."

Jason continued, "This happens to him all the time. Jerome dictates how every game will be played and if we deviate at all from the written rules, he throws a fit and badgers us until no one wants to play anymore. Why can't he let other people set the rules and enjoy the game? Why does everything need to be 'his way'?"

*Interpreting behavior through an Asperger's lens*
MY CHILD IS TRYING TO MAKE HIS CHAOTIC
WORLD FEEL MORE PREDICTABLE

Our children aren't trying to be problematic. They're trying to make their world more predictable. While other children enjoy changing the rules of a game to make it more interesting, our children tend to think in absolutes—feeling anxious when peers deviate from the established guidelines. When they appear inflexible, it's often because they haven't imagined that another option exists. In their universe, there is the right way, or the wrong way, with nothing in between. Our children are not purposefully trying to be difficult, but they do have great difficulty learning how to compromise or accept interpretations that differ from their own.

We confuse them when we change plans, alter schedules, or make requests that catch them off guard. Our children feel more secure when they know what is going to happen and what they have to do. It's easy to interpret their reactions as "over-the-top," but their sensitivity to change, transition, and surprise is predictable given their neurology.

## Consider generalization of skills

One of the most confusing aspects of parenting children with Asperger's is that they can be both knowledgeable about what they are supposed to do and completely incapable of doing it when it's most needed—in real places with real people in real time. Why can't they apply these skills across the board? We see them struggle to transfer skills they've learned in a social skills group to their classrooms, playgrounds, and after-school activities. They seem to miss the information that would alert them to the fact that the skills they have learned in one place are useful in other settings.

Sometimes our children do recognize when they are supposed to use a particular social skill they've learned previously. The difficulty generalizing a skill from a small group setting to the real world is that the real world doesn't always come with willing communicative partners or facilitators. This makes it even more challenging for our kids and they can become confused or give up.

When Noah was in elementary school I took the boys to Florida to visit my parents. We were playing in the pool when another family with a boy near Noah's age showed up. Noah was playing on the steps as the boy got in the pool.

"Hi," the boy said as he walked past Noah. Noah didn't look up, but turned his head away and attempted a wave. The boy proceeded to swim around the pool and came back to the steps.

"Hi," Noah said to the boy as he swam past.

"Hi," the boy replied, as he swam away.

Noah walked around the edge of the pool until he was close to the boy again.

"Hi," Noah said again when the boy surfaced and was swimming away.

Noah continued to follow the boy around the pool, not quite swimming, but not staying still either.

"Hi," Noah said when the boy jumped in. The boy gave Noah a confused look and dove under the water again.

Noah had been learning about greetings in his social skill group at school. They had been practicing how you can greet people with words and gestures. But it's so much more complicated to greet people in real life. Noah was trying to use the skills, and he might have had a willing partner to begin with, but the boy lost interest when Noah's "social approach" seemed different.

## Interpreting behavior through an Asperger's lens
MY CHILD DOESN'T REALIZE HOW TO ACT IN THIS SITUATION

"Noah," I called. "Come over here for a minute. I have something I need to tell you."

"What?" Noah asked.

"Honey, I really like how you are trying to talk to this boy," I began. "It was nice that you said 'hi' to him and he said 'hi' back. But I can tell he's a little confused when you keep saying hi to him."

"I want to play with him," Noah said. "He's supposed to ask me to play now. That's how we practiced it in group."

"That makes sense," I said. "But this boy doesn't go to your group so he doesn't know what you were trying to do. Usually kids just say 'hi' to each other once when they first see each other. They don't keep saying 'hi' after the first time. It's not necessary."

"But how will he know that I want to play with him?" Noah asked.

"You can just take the diving rings over and ask if he wants to use them with you," I suggested. "Usually kids just find something to do together like jumping into the pool or playing Marco Polo; they don't say, 'Do you want to play with me?'"

"But I don't want to do diving rings," Noah said. "I just want to talk to him."

"Well, it seems like he's enjoying jumping in the pool," I replied. "I don't think he'll want to just stay still and talk right now."

"Okay, I'll try the diving rings," Noah said surprisingly. "But I'm going to tell him about Pokémon."

"Sure—that's one way kids find out if they like the same games. Just remember to give him time to talk too," I said to Noah's back as he swam away with the diving rings.

We need to remember that our children don't naturally take context into account to help them know how to behave in various settings. When they attempt to generalize skills to new settings, but fall short, our facilitation can help them manage confusing social situations. If they seem disconnected from their surroundings, our prompts can help them recognize what characteristics are similar to other settings or activities they've experienced in the past.

## Consider executive functioning

Our children often struggle with monitoring their own behavior and deploying resources in order to plan, initiate, and complete tasks. They get overwhelmed and often feel "taken by surprise" as they try to figure out how to solve a problem or manage a complex situation. Let's consider how executive functioning challenges impact how we look for a lost item—a common occurrence for most families!

As of this writing, two of my three sons have lost their wallets, one has lost his library card, one is searching for colored pencils to complete a homework assignment, and one may not be allowed back to karate unless he can find his belt. We have a busy house with too many things in it and we often lose something we need. Here's a typical example of how the process of looking for lost items occurs in our home.

"Mom, have you seen my iPod?" Noah asks innocently enough.

"No," I say. "I haven't. How will you look for it?"

"Mom, you need to help me look," Noah says. "You know I'm not good at this."

"I know looking for things you lose can be challenging," I respond. "I will help you think about how to look for your iPod."

"Mom, can't you just look?" Noah asks from the other room. "I really need the iPod to help me do my homework and it takes me longer to find things."

"Noah, let me know when you're ready to start looking," I answer. "I bet together we can figure out where it is."

*Interpreting behavior through an Asperger's lens*

My child will take longer to develop executive functioning skills

Initiating can be hard for our kids. Noah is busy reading on a comfy couch and doesn't want to be frustrated by looking for something he lost. He's usually quite upset with himself for losing it and looking, often unsuccessfully, makes him feel worse. He'd rather I just do it for him. But that won't help him learn how to handle these types of situations. He can do this with some additional guidance and structure.

Still looking for his iPod, Noah begrudgingly stomps into the kitchen where I'm making dinner. "Fine. I'm here. What do we need to do?"

"Well, do you remember the last time you had it?" I ask. "That will help narrow down possibilities."

"I went for a run with it this morning," he said. "I don't remember where I put it down when I came back from my run."

"What do you usually do when you come back from a run?" I asked. "Is there a certain place you like to sit or do you go right up and take a shower?"

"Usually I sit and read in the living room," Noah answered. "But I've looked and I don't see it."

"Well it sounds like we should look in the living room first," I said. "Let's do it together and you show me how you look for things in that space."

We walk into the living room together and Noah does a cursory scan of the area. He quickly adds, "It's not here. Where should we look next?"

The problem many of our children have is that they often don't see what's right in front of them. Noah will say he can't see something and I will see it just a few feet in front of him. It looks like he's looking in the direction, but he still can't see the item. From Sarah Ward, a speech and language pathologist specializing in executive functioning challenges, I've learned how to teach him to "scan a space" or "zoom out" so that he actually looks and registers what he's seeing. Usually this helps him to see the space around him and he often will find what I see once I draw his attention to the area he's missed the first time.

"Noah, that took you about three seconds to decide the iPod wasn't in the room," I say. "Let's start scanning the space— looking on the floor, under furniture and on furniture before we decide it's not here. Which part of the room should we start with first?"

"The couch, since I sit there a lot." Noah starts by looking at the floor in front of the couch and then peers underneath it. He looks at the couch cushions and quickly moves on. Meanwhile, I see the iPod peeking out from between the couch cushions. The very ones he has just looked past.

"Noah come back and zoom out on the sofa," I say. "Sometimes you need to pick up the cushions and look between or underneath them because things can fall between the cracks."

Noah returns and starts picking up the cushions. As he lifts the middle one, his iPod falls with a thud on the floor.

"Thanks Mom!" Noah yelps as he plugs back into his music.

"Not so fast," I say. "Tell me what you will try to do to keep track of your things in the house."

Noah turns away, but can recite what might help.

"When I'm not using my iPod, I need to keep it in my bin."

"What do you do if you can't find it and it's not in your bin?"

"Try to remember where I had it last," he replies. "Zoom out while I look. Keep looking until I find it."

"Okay, that's a good start," I say. "I'm glad you found your iPod. Thanks for sticking with it, even though it was frustrating."

## Consider perspective taking

Penny, mom of 15-year-old Davis, wondered whether or not her son had empathy.

"Davis is usually only concerned about himself. No matter what else is going on in the family, he will make his needs known and expects us all to drop whatever we are doing to help him. I know he's a teenager and so he's likely to be more self-absorbed. But he's been like this his entire life and we get so worn out from his inability to acknowledge that the rest of us have needs, thoughts, and feelings of our own. Here's a typical exchange between Davis and his dad, and sister, Jenna."

"Davis, we're heading to your sister's recital."

"I don't want to go," he yelled from his room.

"We're all going to support your sister," his dad explained. "But we need to leave now."

"I hate recitals," Davis yelled back. "Plus, Jenna's terrible; why would I want to listen to her play?"

"Davis!" his dad yelled. "That's enough! Get in the car and apologize to your sister."

"What did I say?" Davis asked. "She stinks—why should I lie about it?"

"Jenna began to sob and ran to her room," Penny said. "Davis didn't realize he'd said anything hurtful and was mad at his dad for being mad at him. I worry that he doesn't actually care about anybody else. Why is this so hard for him?"

Davis's ability to understand the thoughts, feelings, and expectations of others—his perspective-taking ability—is delayed. It's hard for a child to do what's expected of him when he's not good at understanding what other people might be thinking or feeling. Davis doesn't realize that his sister might be feeling anxious about her recital and that his comments won't help. He is focused on how the situation impacts him and can't, in that moment, step outside his own needs to consider the needs of the rest of his family.

We have to remember that even though perspective taking— or empathy—is delayed, it still exists within our children. They care deeply, but may find it difficult to recognize subtle hints of emotional states and provide a timely empathetic response (Attwood 2007). Perspective-taking challenges often land our children in trouble. They are misunderstood and unfairly criticized for their lack of, or delayed, empathetic response. They are not trying to be insensitive or hurtful. It's hard to make sense of what others might be thinking, feeling, or wanting from you when you don't intuitively wonder about what others are thinking (Winner 2000).

*Interpreting behavior through an Asperger's lens*
MY CHILD IS STILL LEARNING HOW TO RECOGNIZE AND
RESPOND TO OTHERS' THOUGHTS AND FEELINGS
"Davis, please come here," his dad said.

"What now?" he asked.

"I need your help," his dad answered. "Jenna is really upset because she was already nervous about the recital. When you said that she was terrible, you made her feel worse. I don't know if that's what you were going for, but I need you to go apologize and tell her she'll do great."

"I can't do that. She isn't any good," Davis replied matter-of-factly.

"She feels really bad right now, mostly because of what you said," his dad clarified. "I think you're the only one who can help her. Do you really want her to feel bad?"

"No," Davis answered, "But she's not any good and I'm a terrible liar. What can I say that will help?"

"Just tell her you were in a bad mood and took it out on her," his dad suggested. "Tell her she should still go and prove you wrong."

"Well that's true," Davis said. "Plus, I didn't mean to make her feel bad. I just didn't want to go."

"I know," his dad said, "but she was already worried and your words just made her feel worse. Just imagine how nervous you used to get when you had to talk in front of the class. That's how your sister felt about her recital."

"I didn't know," Davis replied, looking at the floor.

We can help our children tune in to the thoughts and feelings of others by pointing out how others might be feeling or what they might be thinking. Making observations about emotional states and thought processes may increase their awareness and fluency regarding the emotional lives of others. Providing this missing information, by thinking out loud about these internal processes, helps our children realize what we are thinking and feeling.

## Consider hidden social rules

There are a lot of hidden social rules that all children and teens are expected to just know (Myles, Schelvan, and Trautman 2004). We assume that as kids grow up they will learn these implied rules because they watch the world around them, observe how people react and respond, and use that information to guide their own choices and behavior. The difference is that children and teens with Asperger's don't learn by observation and maturation alone. Usually they are not assessing their environment and picking up subtle social cues, correctly interpreting them, and acting on them. If they're missing the incidental learning that's occurring all around them, how will they learn and practice using social behavior? We need to translate the unwritten rules into a language that makes sense.

Let's return to our topic night and hear which behaviors concern Sharon, mom of 14-year-old Kyle.

"We were having a family barbecue at our house," Sharon began. "I'd talked to Kyle about it ahead of time, letting him know who was coming over and when he'd need to join us outside. He said he would and then when his grandparents, aunts, uncles, and cousins showed up, we couldn't get him off the computer. We were all outside telling stories and joking around and he was inside watching anime videos. I got so frustrated I made him come outside and that's when it went from frustrating to mortifying."

"Kyle, you need to come outside now and be with us," Sharon said. "Everyone is outside and you need to join us."

"I don't want to," Kyle replied. "I'm not going."

"Kyle, I will not ask you again," Sharon insisted. "I am telling you to go outside."

Kyle stomped onto the patio. He reached over his grandmother, grabbing chips, and then walked around the backyard with earbuds in his ears. Sharon tried again to lure Kyle back to the group.

"Kyle I want you to join us at the tables," Sharon pleaded. "Please don't go off by yourself."

"This is boring," Kyle replied in too loud a voice so that everyone could hear. "No one is talking about anything interesting."

"Kyle!" Sharon hissed in a stage whisper as he stormed away. Why did Kyle have to say things that could be hurtful to others?

Sharon didn't understand why he couldn't just join the group for a few minutes.

Our hidden social rules and behavioral expectations made it look as if Kyle was being selfish. But misunderstanding social expectations could cause his misbehavior. Kyle couldn't be flexible and take his mother's perspective into account. It doesn't mean he won't ever be able to, but it wasn't going to happen at the family barbecue.

### Interpreting behavior through an Asperger's lens

MY CHILD IS MISSING INFORMATION THAT
OTHERS SEEM TO KNOW IMPLICITLY

Whenever you catch yourself wondering, "Why is he doing that?" or thinking, "I shouldn't have to tell you that!" you probably have a situation where your child is missing the hidden social rules. So often, when we are confused by our child's behavior it is because we haven't adequately explained an important social understanding. Usually we aren't even aware of what they might not know because we learned the social rules implicitly. Don't assume that your child knows what to do and will be able to demonstrate the behavior in a new situation, especially with new people and subtle or nuanced circumstances. Rule-laden situations like funerals, work-related family events, lifecycle events, and school performances all contain prescribed behavioral expectations that our children need help navigating.

## Consider social pragmatics

Social pragmatics is the use of language in a social context (Attwood 2007). Our children usually struggle with recognizing and interpreting nonverbal communication. If we don't make our intentions clear with words (spoken and written), our children miss the nonverbal cues we send their way. That's why they don't stop talking when we sigh heavily, or realize we are about to yell when we give them the evil eye. Not only do they not pick up on the nonverbal communication of others, they don't realize when they are sending negative signals out to peers or adults. Their tone of voice may suggest disgust when they are only in disagreement. Their voice volume may make others feel that they are angry, when they are just speaking loudly and quickly. When they provide monologues instead of dialogues and don't include others in a conversation, they can be seen as rude or insensitive. They are missing the implied rules of social engagement, and they suffer as a result.

Back at our parent topic night on behavior, Joe, a parent of third-grade twin girls, talked about how Amanda, his daughter with Asperger's, confuses other children.

"Amanda loves all things Harry Potter," Joe explained. "All she wants to do is talk about Harry Potter 24/7. But her twin sister, Jessica, gets tired of it. So do the other kids at school and they're starting to make fun of her. Amanda will go up to other classmates and just start talking about Harry Potter. It doesn't matter what the other kids are doing, she'll just start talking, loudly, and it's hard to get her to stop. Jessica's embarrassed and the kids are sending all kinds of signals that should tell Amanda to stop talking, but she doesn't see it." Why is this so hard for Amanda?

Social cognition doesn't come naturally to Amanda. She doesn't pick up all the nonverbal messages her peers are sending. She doesn't realize that they are rolling their eyes, turning away from her, smirking, or wanting to change the subject. She often seems out of sync with social interactions. Amanda has to learn about social communication and how to use it to promote positive interactions with others.

## Interpreting behavior through an Asperger's lens
MY CHILD IS STILL LEARNING HOW TO INTERACT WITH OTHERS
Our children do not acquire social pragmatics as easily as they learn facts about their special interest. They have to be reminded of how to use the complex language of social pragmatics. It is impossible to supply the rules, and their exceptions, for every social situation our children may encounter. But we can point

out the relevant contextual cues to help them recognize how to respond (Vermeulen 2012).

Remember how hard it is to learn a language that doesn't come naturally to you? Did it help when other people got upset with you as you were learning? Applying social knowledge to a dynamic social situation is incredibly challenging. If your child responds well to it, use humor to help manage the innate stress that comes from trying to teach and practice a largely intuitive process in a more systematic way. Effectively using social pragmatics is demanding and exhausting. Please take the time to acknowledge the effort your child is exerting to learn this new language.

## Consider self-awareness and self-advocacy

Our children will be better understood if they are able to explain their needs to others. When peers and adults witness our children's unexpected behavior, they create their own explanations. To avoid incorrect assumptions about their behavior, our children need to understand their strengths and needs, and the strategies and accommodations that help. When our children are young, we advocate on their behalf without having them participate in the process. But how will they understand how their brains and bodies work if we don't help them learn about the role Asperger's plays in their lives?

At a recent topic night, Molly, parent of 11-year-old Eric, shared a story about her son.

"Eric came home from school and threw his backpack on the floor." Molly began. "I almost didn't want to know what set him off this time. He's so easily frustrated and seems really upset with us when we don't know what he's thinking. So I asked what was wrong."

"I can't believe how stupid everyone is at school!" Eric answered. "I understand the math in two seconds, but we have to go over it anyway. Why is everyone else so stupid?"

"Honey—math does come more easily to you, but that doesn't mean other kids are stupid because they need more time or help," Molly responded, trying not to think of Eric as a narcissistic dictator.

"But it's a waste of time," Eric continued. "And I hate being pulled out of class to go to the speech teacher's group. Why do I have to go?"

Molly addressed the group, "I froze when he asked why he had to go. What am I supposed to say? I haven't told him about Asperger's and I'm not sure that will help. I'm afraid he's going to think there's something wrong with him if I bring it up and talk about all the help he needs. But I feel like he shoots himself in the foot every time he opens his mouth. He's so quick to point out everyone else's foibles, but doesn't see any of his own. He's going to alienate all the kids *and* the teachers and then who will help him when he needs it?"

## Interpreting behavior through an Asperger's lens

ASPERGER'S IS NOTHING TO BE ASHAMED OF NOR IS IT AN EXCUSE

Self-awareness and self-advocacy will help our children understand themselves. Keeping information from them does not shelter them from pain or misunderstanding. We can let our children know that they don't need to be a different person for us to love them. It's also important that they learn which situations, activities, areas of interest, strategies or accommodations work well for them. We want to plant the seed of acceptance from an early age so that they don't grow up feeling that they were never good enough.

Sometimes parents worry that once children learn about how Asperger's affects their abilities, they might "give up" and use Asperger's as an excuse when they don't want to do something that's hard for them. When my children have said that they can't do something due to their diagnosis and the challenges it brings, I respond with the following, "I know it is harder for you to do this. It may take you longer and you may have to learn it differently, but that doesn't mean you can't try or that you won't ever be able to do it." My children are more willing to try something that's hard for them when I explain that there are many ways to learn a skill and that we will try to teach it in a way that makes sense for them.

## Key tips on interpreting your child's behavior

So, how do we know when a child or teen needs a gentle nudge, clear redirection, consequences, or no response? How do we manage our own feelings about their behavior and the social situations that come with well-entrenched perceptions of what's acceptable and unacceptable?

- *Always consider the context*: We can't analyze social behavior without considering the context in which it occurs. Check your child's understanding of the situation before assuming you understand why they are behaving in a particular way (Vermeulen 2012).

- *Acknowledge and recognize developmental delays*: Erika Drezner, Coordinator of Child and Teen Services at AANE, reminds us about delays in development: "Our kids seem younger because they are younger developmentally." (Drezner 2012, p.12). Although most 10-year-olds may be able to have a sleepover without a stringent list of dos and don'ts, a 10-year-old with Asperger's may need a checklist to help him remember how to stay calm and be a good guest or host. "If we remind ourselves that it is normal for our kids to do things at their own pace and in their own way, we can relieve ourselves of some of the anxiety we feel" (Drezner 2012, p.13).

- *Acknowledge and recognize strengths*: Our children have strengths that also impact their behavior. Some might have a strong sense of truth and justice. Many are intensely loyal to people they care about. Some excel academically. Others have a quirky sense of humor. We have to consider strengths in addition to challenges.

- *Check your assumptions*: Assess whether or not you may have made some false assumptions about what your child is capable of socially and behaviorally. It's easy to interpret our children's behavior as intentionally disrespectful. When we consider how Asperger's may affect their ability to show social competence, we can propose new hypotheses.

- *Apologize when you overreact*: Sometimes our children receive negative feedback from others when they make social mistakes. Teach how to repair relationships and apologize to your child when it is warranted.

- *Manage your own emotions*: Parenting requires a great deal of emotional regulation. Parenting children with Asperger's and related conditions requires more emotional regulation. As we are helping our children learn how to build their capacity to be more socially competent, we might also benefit from help to manage our strong emotions.

- *Acknowledge effort*: Our children have to master the social curriculum in addition to everything else that is expected of them at home and school. They have to exert more effort to be socially competent and it may leave them feeling exhausted and stressed. Let them know you understand how draining it can be to socialize. Give them positive feedback when they go outside their comfort zone and provide a safe space for them to refuel when their energy reserves are low.

## Setting panic aside

It is hard to know what percentage of our child's behavior is due to typical development and what percentage is due to Asperger's. Looking at your child's behavior through an Asperger's lens helps you to parent with compassion, understanding, and patience.

# CHAPTER 3

# Disclosure

*How to Tell Your Child About Asperger's
and When to Consider Telling Others*

We worry that our children will feel bad about themselves if they know about their diagnosis. We're apprehensive about how to tell our children, other family members, or friends about a diagnosis. We're uneasy about labeling our children and wonder if the label will limit them. Sometimes we are concerned that our children will use the diagnosis as an excuse for their behavior or as a way to avoid activities they don't want to do. Although the majority of disclosures have a positive result, most parents feel unsure of when and how to share information related to a diagnosis.

Regardless of whether or not children know their diagnosis, we need to help them understand themselves. Disclosure increases self-awareness, which is a prerequisite for self-advocacy (being able to effectively communicate needs). When our children understand their unique mix of strengths and challenges and the types of accommodations or supports that are helpful, they are more able to manage at home, at school, and out in the larger world.

Throughout their lives, our children get messages that tell them that they need to be different from what comes naturally to them. Sometimes they are told directly that their actions and words need to match the cultural context they are in, whether at school, at a family event, or on a team. We want our children to understand the larger social world, so that they can take part in it. We don't want our children to inadvertently close off options for connecting with the people around them. We need our children to be able to explain how AS affects them. Learning and understanding is reciprocal—we help our children understand the social world, and our children help the larger social world understand them in return.

Throughout this chapter on disclosure, you will learn that:

- self-advocacy begins with young children and continues through the lifespan:

  ◦ how can you help children understand their strengths and challenges?

  ◦ how can you help children and teens communicate their needs?

  ◦ how can you build skills to support self-advocacy at school, at home, and in the community?

- disclosure is an on-going conversation:

  ◦ why disclose to your child?

  ◦ how should you disclose?

  ◦ why tell others?

## Self-advocacy for any age

Parents advocate on their child's behalf at school, at home, and out in the world when children are too young to have the skills to explain themselves. One of the most important skills we teach our children is how to advocate for themselves; let them practice this as often as possible to build their comfort and ability.

*Will I make my child feel bad?*
Lisa, parent of 7-year-old Lizzy, came to the topic night on self-advocacy and disclosure. She was feeling apprehensive about focusing on what was hard for Lizzy because her child already felt bad about herself.

"I don't want to talk to my daughter about what is hard for her," Lisa said. "She already feels like she is bad and that people are mad at her all the time. I feel like if I point it out to her, it will just make her feel worse about herself."

*What can Lisa do to help her young daughter understand herself?*

- *Normalize challenges*: Talk about the challenges of each family member so that your child doesn't feel as if she is the only one who struggles. It's helpful to let your child know if you or someone else in the family had similar difficulties, so that she doesn't feel so alone.

- *Think out loud*: Share how you solve problems and approach challenging situations. It helps your child see that everyone faces dilemmas and needs to think through how to address them.

- *Help your child learn why things are hard*: Your child already knows what is hard for him, even if he can't or hasn't expressed it. What he hasn't learned (maybe) is *why* it is hard, how to ask for help or express his own discomfort or inability, and how to resolve the problem. When your child doesn't have words to express his exhaustion or frustration, he expresses it behaviorally.

- *Read books or watch movies with Asperger's characters*: These might help our children feel less alone as they read about familiar problems, abilities, feelings, and experiences. Kari Dunn Buron's *Adalyn Clare*, explores a fourth grader's relationship with a therapy puppy and would be a good choice for a child with social anxiety (Buron 2012).

- *Use age-appropriate workbooks that teach about Asperger's*: Parents should review books to determine which sections to share with their children. Therapists or social skills group leaders can also help address issues and apply the lessons from the workbooks in an individualized way. Ellen Korin's *Asperger Syndrome: An Owner's Manual* and *Asperger Syndrome: An Owner's Manual 2* are good places to start (Korin 2006, 2007).

## Practicing self-advocacy in a safe environment

Let's return to the topic night on disclosure and hear what Robin, mom of 13-year-old Liam, was concerned about.

"My son is a seventh grader and I don't think that giving him language to express his needs will be enough," she began. "He is used to me doing all the explaining for him and he likes it that way. I don't know how to shift away from doing it for him and helping him learn how to do it for himself. It seems like I do it all and it goes okay or I do nothing and it falls apart. I want him to be able to advocate for himself, but I don't know how to shift."

## How can we conscientiously shift responsibility for advocating from parent to child?

- *Be adaptable*: When parents have been advocating on their child's behalf for years, it can be hard to figure out how to have your child take on a larger role. Let him practice his self-advocacy skills alongside you. Don't drop your support entirely, but hold yourself back from stepping in and completely taking over as he learns and makes mistakes.

- *Teach skills*: Self-advocacy requires explicit teaching. You can teach the skills yourself or have a therapist, speech and language pathologist, other adult, or peer teach them depending on the age of your child. A sample self-advocacy curriculum might include:

  ◦ understanding your strengths and challenges

- ○ understanding which accommodations and supports are useful

- ○ understanding when to advocate

- ○ knowing how to advocate with peers and adults

- ○ problem solving what to do if advocacy doesn't yield needed support

- ○ staying calm through the advocacy process.

- *Provide opportunities to practice*: The more your child gets to practice self-advocacy the better. You want her to practice while she is a child and teen so that when she is an adult, she will be more accustomed to how and when she needs to use these skills. Your child can practice self-advocacy throughout the day by doing any of the following:

- ○ asking to meet with teachers about assignments

- ○ presenting her concerns at team meetings

- ○ asking questions when ordering in a restaurant

- ○ explaining why she would rather not take notes at a meeting or during group work and offering to take on a different role

- ○ explaining to new acquaintances that she paces to feel more comfortable in large groups and that she isn't ignoring them

- ○ letting friends know that if she stands too close, they should tell her because she doesn't always realize when she's making someone uncomfortable.

- *Allow glitches to occur*: It's easy for our kids to experience glitches in their daily life. Although we don't want them to experience challenges that stretch them to the point of breaking, experiencing problems that don't cause their anxiety to skyrocket and that they can manage is important. When our children are able to overcome these challenging incidents, they can build a sense of resilience as they recognize their ability to work through a situation they didn't think was manageable. We don't want to rid our children of complications they can cope with, because as adults we want them to have experiences to draw from. Use glitches as an opportunity to practice problem solving in a safe environment.

## Disclosure—an on-going conversation with your child

### Stigma attached to autism spectrum diagnosis

When our children have a medical diagnosis, like diabetes or asthma, we don't blame them for the symptoms and side effects that go along with the condition. We also don't tend to feel that we can't tell others. But a diagnosis of Asperger's or autism spectrum is different because it affects our child's ability to function socially. Social communication and social behavior are integral parts of everything we do with others. Each social situation our children encounter has contextual expectations attached to it (Vermeulen 2012). Our children routinely breach these social norms as a symptom and consequence of their neurology. Their inadvertent violation of social expectations may lead to undeserved, but understandable, negative responses from those around them.

There are also misconceptions about children with Asperger's. When people hear the term Asperger's or autism spectrum they imagine that our children are antisocial. In fact, many of our children want friends, but don't know how to initiate and maintain these relationships. Sometimes people assume a child with Asperger's is either very disabled or doesn't really need any help because they are "little geniuses." The reality is that our children require different amounts and types of help depending on the situation and setting. Our children can be completely capable in certain situations, and also need intense help in others. As my son explained once when asked if he needed an assistant in school, "I need help when I need it, and I don't when I don't." And that's what adds to the misunderstandings about Asperger's—we more easily understand our children when they are consistent—and yet children with Asperger's are consistently inconsistent.

Before you can talk with your child about Asperger's or the autism spectrum, you have to be comfortable with the term and diagnosis. If you feel that having Asperger's is shameful, that will come across in your explanation to your child. If you feel devastated or sad and get tearful each time you think or talk about it, you may need more time before raising it with your child. Many parents have a range of emotions about their child's diagnosis. For some it provides validation and clarity after years of confusion. For others it can bring up fears and uncertainty as they try to integrate this new information into their understanding of their child. Talking to other parents and getting information to help you understand AS can help.

### When is it time to have "the talk"?

Allison, mom of 10-year-old Nolan, came to the topic night wondering when to talk to him about Asperger's.

"Nolan got his diagnosis two years ago," she said. "He seemed pretty oblivious to how other people treated him and so we didn't see a need to talk to him about Asperger's then. But recently he's been noticing that some of the kids in his class who used to play with him at recess don't want to anymore. When he tries to talk to them, they run away from him. Nolan's teacher said that his classmates don't like to be his partner in gym because he's always picking his nose in plain sight before they have to hold hands for the dance unit. I feel so bad for him and I want him to be more aware of how he acts around other people. It seems like it might be time to talk to him, but how do I know if I'm right?" Allison's concerns resonated with the other parents in the room. They were looking for parameters to indicate when they would know it was time to disclose to their child.

## How will you know when it is time to talk with your child about Asperger's?

- *Your child asks*: Sometimes a child will see a book or overhear a conversation and ask you directly.

- *Your child is confused*: Sometimes a child will ask why other kids no longer include them or wonder why other children struggle with concepts they find simple. This provides the opportunity to talk about strengths and challenges and give this mixture of attributes a name.

- *Your child is approaching adolescence*: It helps to have this information before adolescence. Many parents find that grade four or five in elementary (primary) school is a better time to start the conversation rather than waiting until middle or high (secondary) school (if you know).

- *Your child is labeling himself*: Sometimes children will start to think or say that they are hyper, stupid, bad, or lazy. They will internalize the labels others put on them. It is better for them if they have accurate information and understand that their difficulties are due to their neurology, not an inherent character defect.

- *You want to tell others*: If you are going to tell other children, your own child will need to know too. Once you share the information with others, there is always the chance someone will share it with your child before you do.

- *School or a clinician suggests it*: Learn more about what your child is doing or saying in those settings to prompt the request. You can also disclose with their assistance.

## How to disclose to your child

Let's rejoin our topic night and hear from Maria, mom of 11-year-old Alicia.

"I know it's probably time to tell my daughter, but I don't know how," she said. "I don't want her to think that Asperger's is bad or that she is bad because she has it. How do I make sure that doesn't happen?"

Many parents feel this way. They realize it's time to disclose because their child is having more difficulties. When we believed it was time for us to disclose to Noah, because he was asking a lot of questions and noticing how he was different from other children in his class, I sought out counsel from another AANE mom. She had gone through this process the year before and shared an example of how she talked with her child. Her template helped me imagine how I could do this with my own child.

The actual disclosure with the label of Asperger's or ADHD went more smoothly than I anticipated with my children. When Noah was in grade four, he started showing the signs that we needed to move the conversation from his strengths and challenges and provide more information to help him understand why certain things were difficult for him and other things that seemed so easy to him were stressful for others. I started by setting an appointment in a comfortable space at home.

"Noah, remember how we've always talked about your strengths—things that come very easily to you—and your challenges—things that seem really difficult or that you aren't interested in?" I asked. "Why don't we make a list on paper so that we can both remember some from each category?"

As Noah and I made the list, shown in Table 3.1, I made sure to include many things from the strengths category and tried not to overwhelm him with the challenges he was currently showing.

**Table 3.1**: Characteristics of Asperger's

| Strengths | Challenges |
| --- | --- |
| Loyal | Understanding other people |
| Honest | Talking to other people |
| Great memory for things that interest me | Handwriting |
| Science is easy for me | Organizing my schoolwork |

Taking the time to use a visual helped to slow down the conversation. Also, when you feel nervous about something, it's easy to ramble on and overwhelm your child as you babble away. Writing the list helped keep the conversation focused, calm, and moving at a reasonable pace.

"Noah, there are many children and adults in the world who also share this list of strengths and challenges; there's actually a name for it," I continued. "Would you like to know what it is?"

"Okay," he answered.

"It's called Asperger's," and before I could say anything further, he started to laugh.

"What kind of name is that?" he continued through his chortles.

"I know it's a funny name," I responded. "It's actually the last name of the doctor who figured out what this mix of characteristics was. His name was Hans Asperger—the diagnosis was named after him."

"I would change my name," Noah said.

"Noah, even with the funny name, the diagnosis doesn't change who you are," I continued. "You are still the same person you were before we had this talk. But I hope it helps to explain why you struggle with certain things, like understanding what others are thinking or feeling, or handwriting, and why certain things come so easily to you, but not to others, like science and remembering details for things that interest you."

When Noah didn't chime in, I continued, "Having Asperger's means that you might need to learn some things in a different way or it may take you more or less time to learn something than the kids around you. It's not good or bad to have Asperger's. It's just a part of who you are, like having blue eyes or red hair. Does that make sense?"

"Do we know anybody else who has it?" he asked.

"Well, many people speculate that some famous people from history had Asperger's," I shared, knowing that he would find this interesting. "One of them is Albert Einstein. The kids in your group after school also have Asperger's." I had asked the parents ahead of time if I could share this information, and they had given their consent.

"That's cool," he replied.

"Do you have any questions?" I asked thinking that was probably enough for our first talk.

"No," he replied looking through his graphic novel. "Can I read now?"

"Sure, honey," I answered. "We can talk about this anytime. I love you."

It can be hard to know when you've said enough but not too much. I equate the disclosure talk with the sex education talk. You provide small amounts of information in a short amount of time. You listen. You ask if they have questions. You try to share information in a developmentally appropriate way so that you don't overwhelm them. You are setting the stage for future conversations about Asperger's.

Although I had the initial disclosure conversation when Noah was 10, we've continued to have many more discussions about Asperger's and the autism spectrum in the seven years since. It's as normal a topic of conversation as our talks about our dog, homework, movies, food, and books. Asperger's and autism have been built into the fabric of our family and aren't something to be embarrassed about or shy away from. This is what disclosure can do for families—it takes a topic that people are worried about, shines some light on it, and makes it more familiar. Secrets in a family breed a sense of shame. Disclosure takes away that negative connotation.

*How to disclose to your adolescent—additional considerations*
Whenever possible, it is easier to disclose before your child is an adolescent. However, for some families that isn't an option because they don't have a diagnosis or the parents or the child aren't ready. Even if you don't have a diagnosis in the earlier years or don't feel ready to disclose a diagnosis you do have, it's helpful to talk about strengths and challenges so that your child gets exposed to the language and ideas. Teenagers don't want to

examine their challenges (especially with parents), so how can you handle disclosure if you have an adolescent?

- *Timing matters*: Make an appointment to have a short conversation when it works for your child. Don't pull them away from activities they enjoy to have "the talk."

- *Language matters*: Let your teen know that you are sharing this information so that she can better understand how she learns. Don't focus on all the struggles your child has, but offer a balanced conversation, with more focus on her strengths. No adolescent wants to be reminded about her challenges a parent.

- *Share experiences*: If other adults in the family or friends share some of the same struggles, share those experiences and stories with your teen so he knows he isn't alone.

- *Connect to other teens*: Some teens start or continue these conversations through small groups at school or privately. Sometimes peer mentors at school can provide information and perspective.

- *Adult involvement*: Parents don't have to have the conversation alone with their teen. Therapists, teachers, and other trusted adults could be involved.

## How to help teens think about their diagnosis

Sherri came to the topic night on disclosure worried that her 16-year-old son, Alex, would never accept his diagnosis or the help he needed.

"Alex doesn't realize what he doesn't know," she began. "He thinks he will be able to get through college, get a job and live on his own without any help. He's living in a fantasy world. He has never volunteered anywhere or gotten a job. He is barely passing his classes. He needs to be reminded every day about what he needs to do. His teachers are constantly after him to turn in his work. He has no idea what he needs and rejects any help offered at school or home. How will he manage?"

Often during the teen years, adolescents do not want to admit that they need help with anything. That's why a diagnosis that highlights a deficit can feel threatening.

### How do we convince secondary students to accept or seek out the necessary assistance?

- *Evaluate what's working*: Ask your teen to evaluate or rate challenging areas to assess what's working. A teen coming to the decision on his own is much better than a parent telling him what he needs to do.

- *Trial basis*: If you are asking your teen to do something differently, set a short-term trial basis so that he knows you aren't changing something indefinitely.

- *WIIFM (What's in it for me?)*: Focus on what motivates your teen and discuss the benefits of a new approach. How does addressing his challenges make your teen's life easier? For some teens, the only thing that motivates them is having people leave them alone. Explain that when they try out a support or strategy, they will get pestered less by parents and other adults.

- *Problem solve together*: Instead of getting stuck in arguing opposing points of view about what is needed, listen to your teen, validate her point of view and discuss how you can work together to address any challenges. Sometimes this might mean that the teen agrees to work with someone other than the parent to solve the problem.

- *Use incentives*: Coming to terms with your challenges is hard work for all teens. Sometimes incentives or rewards help get adolescents over their resistance to change and allow them to try something new.

# Disclosing to other people

*Our children are disclosing, inadvertently, all the time*

Let's rejoin the topic night on self-advocacy and disclosure and hear from Jim, parent of 9-year-old Charlie. He felt strongly that Charlie could "pass" as neurotypical and wondered why he should focus on his son's challenges.

"Charlie's a really smart boy," Jim began. "Every doctor and teacher tells us he's very 'high functioning.' He's well ahead of all his classmates in almost all subjects. Kids don't ask to play with him, he sits by himself at lunch, and during recess he reads. I guess I'm wondering how helping him understand what's hard for him will help. I assumed as he got older and the academic work grew more challenging, he would connect to other kids more easily. I'm not sure that any of his classmates can tell that he has challenges. I think they just think he's a smart boy." Why would Jim teach Charlie about his social interaction challenges? How does this help Charlie?

Children with Asperger's are disclosing all the time. Neurotypical children notice when classmates behave in bewildering ways. They wonder why a child is talking or acting in a surprising manner. They feel confused and will come up with their own label to make sense of puzzling behavior. This happens to many of our children who get branded as "weird" or "strange" because their classmates don't understand them.

*How do our children "disclose" without intending to do so?*

- Having meltdowns at school.
- Using a loud voice in the classroom.
- Being inflexible when working in a group.
- Not joining in at recess or lunch.
- Doing "private" behaviors in public (nose picking, masturbation).
- Pacing in the classroom.

- Standing or sitting too close to others.

- Using classmates' supplies without asking.

- Using a keyboard or other assistive technology device.

- Talking about a special interest even when others show their disinterest.

- Not picking up on teacher's nonverbal communication.

- Chewing on clothing or gum.

- Their nonverbal communication seems "off."

It is better for our children to understand and be able to express their strengths, challenges, and needs to others than it is for others to make up their own unflattering explanations. Whether your child uses the term Asperger's, autism spectrum, or no label at all, classmates tend to be more helpful and less exclusionary, when they know why someone is behaving in a perplexing way and what they can do or say to help.

### Disclosing to classmates—when is your child ready?
Once our children have a better sense of their own strengths and challenges, and how their Asperger's or autism spectrum diagnosis affects them, they may want to share this information with their classmates. Your child may be ready to do this if she is comfortable with talking to her class, has the help of a teacher to figure out what to say, has a generally supportive classroom, and understands why this type of information sharing is important. Many students do this around grade four or five. Once children move on to middle and high school the information sharing is more individualized and not typically done as a full class or school.

When my son was in grade four, we moved from New Jersey to Massachusetts. Since none of the other children grew up with him, they weren't used to his idiosyncrasies. Toward the end of his grade four year, with the help of his special education teacher, he put together a presentation about how Asperger's affects him.

The key aspects of the short presentation to his class included:

- explaining Asperger's
- talking about his own strengths
- talking about some challenges
- being clear about how others could help.

Noah's presentation ended with a Q&A session. One of the children asked, "Is there a cure for Asperger's?"

Noah responded without glancing at his teacher, "You don't need a cure," he said. "It's not a disease." His point was clear. Asperger's was something you needed to understand so that you could provide support and accommodations—it was not something you needed to eradicate.

### Disclosing to community programs

At a recent topic night on disclosure, Becky was wondering if she needed to explain Asperger's to the summer camp where she wanted to send her 12-year-old son, Will.

"There's this wonderful camp my older children went to when they were Will's age," Becky said. "But I'm afraid they won't take Will if they know he has Asperger's. Do we have to tell them? Can't we just send him and hope the homey atmosphere and caring staff will be the right fit? I don't want him to miss out on the experience."

If a camp, school, child-care, or after-school program won't take your child because they have an Asperger's or autism spectrum diagnosis, I'd be cautious about sending them. If any of these types of places say they are not equipped to handle a child on the spectrum, then chances are that they are not the right place—even if they worked for your other children. It is helpful to be clear about your child's challenges and the strategies that work for him, even if you do not share the actual diagnosis. You can't expect a program to work well with your child if you don't let them know about potential challenges and what has worked in the past. Although you can share the diagnosis, that alone won't tell the program what your child needs. To be more specific, include a "helpful hints" sheet to clarify what will help your child succeed in their setting (see Figure 3.1).

### Disclosing to other parents

Back at our topic night, Bruce, parent of 9-year-old Ben, wondered how he should tell other parents about Ben's needs.

"We just moved to a new neighborhood and everyone is very friendly," Bruce said. "Ben was diagnosed with Asperger's last year. Lots of neighborhood kids are coming over or inviting Ben over to play. Do we need to say anything to the kids or their parents? Ben has never had so many kids around and I can already see the confused looks on their faces when they play at our house. Sometimes we have a bunch of neighborhood kids playing in the backyard while Ben sorts out his Pokémon cards. What should we do?"

Should Bruce "disclose" to his new neighbors?

### How do you know if you should tell other parents?

- *Your child's behavior confuses other parents*: You don't have to give a diagnosis, but may want to share clarifying information. Examples might include any of the following:

  - "Ben likes to share a lot of information about Pokémon cards. If you get tired of hearing about it, you just have to tell him you want to talk about something else. He doesn't realize when other people might want to change the topic of conversation or are bored."

  - "Ben does better when he knows what to expect. Telling him the schedule, and letting him know if it needs to be altered, helps. Writing it down or using timers helps him with the changes too."

  - "If Ben seems upset because something changed, could you remind him to take a break until he feels better?"

Dear _____

The information included here is to help you understand, work with, and enjoy my child, _____. Thank you for taking the time to read this and incorporating successful strategies and approaches when needed. The most important things to know about my child are:

- Most difficult behaviors are *not willful or intentionally oppositional*. They are the result of his neurological condition. My child may be overwhelmed, anxious or confused about what you expect from him.

- Using the strategies on this sheet will help improve my child's behavior.

- If you can incorporate my child's special interests into an activity, he is more likely to cooperate and be involved successfully. His special interests include _____
_____.

- Please be clear, specific, and concrete with your directions and explain briefly why they should be followed.

- In a distress situation, *please don't touch, or talk to my child. Provide a safe space for him to calm down and his strong reaction will pass.* Please let us know about any situations like this.

Best hints to use with my child are:

- Provide a visual schedule.

- If my child can be in a group with kids with similar interests that may help. Please do not place him with highly competitive or athletic kids.

- Allow my child to chew gum or sour candies during group activities.

- Please have a counselor help facilitate social interactions.

- Allow breaks.

**Figure 3.1**: Helpful hints for my child

- *Parents are making incorrect assumptions*: When parents misinterpret or misunderstand your child's needs, it can be helpful to provide information to clarify why your child behaves as she does.

  ○ "Penny isn't trying to be annoying to your daughter by standing too close to her. She has a hard time figuring how much space everyone needs. If your daughter holds her arm out to show Penny, she'll move back."

  ○ "Laurel isn't trying to bug your son by hugging him. She still thinks hugging all her classmates is the way you tell them you like them and want to play. You can remind her that high-fives can replace hugs."

  ○ "When George walks away from you when you are talking to him, he doesn't realize you still wanted to say more. Just let him know you still need his attention. He might need to move around while he listens and he probably won't look at you, but if you ask him to repeat what you just said, he usually can."

## Disclosing to family members

Janna came to the parent topic night on disclosure wondering whether she should tell her family about 5-year-old Tanner's diagnosis of AS.

"My family thinks I worry too much about Tanner. Whenever I've tried to talk with them about his challenges they tease me and change the subject. Last week I was at my sister, Melanie's, house and I tried again."

"Melanie, I don't think Tanner has any friends at school," Janna began. "I drive by at recess and I see him walking around the playground talking to himself."

"Janna, you worry too much," Melanie responded predictably. "Tanner's fine and why does it matter if he's walking around the playground by himself?"

"He doesn't know how to make friends," Janna answered. "He's never going to have a buddy."

"Of course he will—when he's ready," Melanie said. "You need to stop seeing a problem where there isn't one."

"I don't think my family will believe me," Janna explained. "I'm also worried that they might give me all kinds of unhelpful advice. How do I tell them?"

Just as every child with Asperger's is unique—so is every family. You know how your family tends to respond to unique needs of individual members.

To help you decide when and how to tell your family, consider the following:

- *Identify your allies*: Start by telling family members who have been supportive in the past. It's easier to share difficult information if you don't have the added burden of convincing your listener that the diagnosis is real.

- *Tailor your message*: If you think a particular family member will struggle to digest the information, provide small amounts to start and consider the vocabulary you use. Although your overall message will be the same, the details and focus may change depending on your audience.

- *Clarify your needs*: If you would like your family to listen without offering suggestions, let them know. You might sound defensive if you make this statement after advice is presented.

- *Be ready for a range of responses*: Sometimes your family will respond just as you'd hoped. At other times, they may say things you find offensive. Or they may need you to take care of their emotional response. Remember that this is new information that they may not have been expecting. Give everyone time to adjust.

### Sometimes siblings want a diagnosis too

I was driving in the car with my three boys a few years ago, and we were talking about Tim Page's book, *Parallel Play* (Page 2009). Page is an accomplished writer and music critic, and an adult with Asperger's. At the time Noah was interested in writing and movies and so I was telling him about the book in case he wanted to read it. In the middle of our conversation Josh asked, "Do I have Asperger's?"

"It's okay if you have Asperger's," Noah replied without missing a beat. "There's nothing wrong with that."

Josh had more inquiries. "Do I have ADHD?" he pondered aloud.

"It's okay if you have ADHD," Daniel replied quickly. "Lots of really creative people have it."

And before Josh could ask about any other diagnoses he might add to his personal description, I added, "It's okay if you don't have either." I was glad that Noah and Daniel were feeling positive about their own diagnoses, but I wanted Josh to know that he didn't need to have a diagnosis to fit into our family.

What helped our family reach this level of comfort was normalizing Asperger's and ADHD. We may have gone too far, as evidenced by Josh's inquiry, but not having a stigma attached to these labels has helped us tremendously. That's not to say that there haven't been many moments when we wondered if we said the right thing in terms of disclosure, especially in the beginning.

## Setting panic aside

Our anxiety about disclosure makes sense. We don't want to do the wrong thing. We don't want to say anything that makes our children hurt. We need to remember that our own responses to the diagnosis and the process we go through is different from what our children experience. The range of responses varies and we don't know if our children will think it is "no big deal" or if they will want to research all there is to know about the topic. The best we can do is be calm, listen, offer ways to gather information, and recognize that disclosure is a process. Some days our children will feel fine about themselves and their diagnoses and other days they might not. We can offer a safe place to bring their emotions and questions as they figure out what Asperger's means to them.

# CHAPTER 4 ————————————————

# Friendship Foundations

We all have our own experiences with friendship. If we're lucky, we know what it feels like to discover a good fit with a person and have a friendship that blossoms. We've probably also experienced what it feels like to initiate a friendship only to have the other person not reciprocate or turn out to be a poor choice.

When we were young, our parents and teachers conveyed the importance of being respectful, taking turns, and apologizing when we were in the wrong. They may have stayed away from our conflicts with friends, telling us to work it out on our own. Through trial and error we discovered which friends were a good fit for us. And if we were fortunate, we experienced how a good friend can help us feel better, make celebrations more gratifying, and increase the pleasure of experiences through shared interest.

But our kids won't learn solely through experience. We need to be explicit and systematic about teaching what it means to be and have a friend. We can't expect that it will happen for them without structure and support in the beginning. We have to anticipate that not every attempt will lead to a successful friendship. We need to understand what contributes to our children's difficulty with making friends and how we can support their desire to connect.

Throughout this chapter on friendship, you will learn about:

- how to cope with the emotional impact of social isolation or rejection:
  - parent and child responses
  - connecting to others who understand
- the hidden curriculum of friendship:
  - explaining friendship
  - making and keeping friends
- how Asperger's affects your child's friendships:
  - emotional regulation
  - perspective taking
  - social pragmatics.

## Emotional impact of social isolation and rejection

One of our topic nights on friendship started out with Scott, father of 10-year-old Michael, crying as he choked out why he had come to the parent group.

"My son has no friends," Scott said. "Nobody invites Michael anywhere. None of the kids in our neighborhood seek him out. He walks out of school alone. We've tried groups and activities, but Michael doesn't make a connection. I feel like a complete failure as a dad and my son feels like a failure too."

### Dealing with our own emotions and expectations

Before we can talk about the ways we try to help kids meet potential friends, we need to address the strong emotions we feel as parents whose children struggle to connect with other children. It is upsetting to watch your child make overtures, only to be rejected. It is also painful to watch other children effortlessly play together on the playground, while your child sits on the sidelines. I can remember encountering a group of parents gathered outside the elementary school at pick up time talking about a class pool party that afternoon. The entire class had been invited, except for my son. It was as if he and I were both invisible.

It's all too easy to feel isolated, sad, and exhausted as a parent of a child who struggles with making social connections. Typical children who seem to connect with one another so easily surround us. How different the lives of our children are! But we can build in buffers and make connections to lessen the sting. Still, there will be instances that highlight how much harder it is for our children to make friends—and when that happens, we feel deflated.

When my oldest son was in elementary school, one of his classmate's moms chatted with me as we walked home from dropping off our children at school.

"I just wanted to tell you how happy I am that Luke is in class with Noah," she said warmly.

"I'm sure Noah feels the same way," I replied, feeling a kinship starting to grow between us. I imagined an offer for the ever-elusive play date might be next.

"It's such a good experience for Luke to be with a child on the spectrum," she continued. "I think it's important for him to be around someone with Asperger's."

I'm not often speechless, but that comment caught me off guard. I didn't want Noah to be seen as a "good experience." I wanted Noah to be understood and appreciated for who he was. I hoped that others would see Noah as a whole human being and a potential friend. Yet this mom labeled Noah as a non-entity; she would always think of Noah as something rather than someone.

My child doesn't make me sad. What does is seeing how the world sometimes reacts to him. Some judge him for the social mistakes he makes, even though he is capable of being a good friend. Some parents have guided their own children away from him when they show an interest. It is okay to feel dispirited or angry with any of these experiences. We can't change the experience, but we can connect to others who know what it's like to have a child who is disconnected at times.

### Dealing with our children's emotions

Listen to Renee's concerns about her 9-year-old daughter Emma and her classmates.

"Emma will go up to the girls and start talking about her American Girl dolls non-stop. The other girls in the class seem very mean. They roll their eyes and call Emma names, but Emma seems oblivious to it. Part of me is glad that she doesn't notice how people feel about her, because then she won't feel rejected. I don't think I can point it out to her. It feels cruel to tell your child that other children find them annoying and don't want to be with them. But won't she notice some day and feel hurt to realize she doesn't have the friends she thought she did?"

Many parents feel relieved when their children seem unaware of their peers' negative reactions. We often feel the outrage more strongly than our children.

Even when children appear unaware of the responses around them, it helps to instill the following messages:

- *You are learning to be a friend*: It takes lots of practice to become a good friend to others. Let your child know she is learning how to do that and as she is learning she will make some mistakes and that is okay.

- *You are loved just the way you are*: Let your child know that he is loved "as is." He does not have to be a better friend to earn your love.

- *Other children and adults are also learning how to be a good friend*: Just because a child or adult is not on the autism spectrum, it does not mean that they have stellar friendship skills. Other people make mistakes too. We all have to be patient with each other.

- *Adults can help*: If your child feels threatened or bullied by others, she needs to tell a trusted adult. No child should endure bullying or harassment.

### Dealing with our children's emotions when they are more aware of social rejection and exclusion

As children get older, they often become more aware of how others are treating them. This is an important development, but it's also a painful one. My family experienced this during the middle school years.

Noah came home more agitated than usual. While he was having a snack, he started talking. "Something weird has been happening all week. Whenever I sit down at my regular lunch table, all the other kids get up and walk away to another table. So I get up and walk over to the new table too. As soon as I sit with them and open my lunch, they get up and move again to another table. This happened four times and then I finally gave up and just stayed at the table by myself. Why are they doing that?" he asked, truly perplexed by the confusing situation.

My first thought was, "Because they are jerks," but I kept that to myself. Instead I tried to help him understand the situation and think about how to get help to stop it from happening again.

"That does sound very confusing," I said. "I'm sorry that happened to you. Why do you think these kids kept moving to another table as soon as you sat down?"

"I don't know," he replied. "I wouldn't do that to anybody. It's weird and mean."

"I agree. It sounds like these kids decided to exclude you from the group. I don't know why they did it, but it's wrong," I said clearly. "Since this happened at school, I bet one of your teachers would be able to help. I'm sure the school doesn't want kids to treat each other this way. Do you think we could write an email together to see how we could make this better?"

"I don't want to get them in trouble," he said. "I thought they were my friends."

"Honey, if they are doing this to you, that's not being a good friend," I clarified. "Sometimes kids like to play tricks on each other, but this sounds like more than that. This is mean-spirited and exclusionary."

"But they are my friends," Noah repeated.

I had a lump in my throat as I tried to explain what was happening, "I think they are more like classmates, not friends. It sounds like they are people you know well from being in classes together, but not necessarily because you hang out together after school. I'm sorry that they are treating you this way. It's not right. I think we should write the email so that things can start getting better at school. This is the kind of situation that requires help from teachers. How about I start it and then you can make sure it doesn't say anything that makes you uncomfortable?" I asked.

Noah nodded in agreement. I hated that I had to point out that he was being excluded on purpose, but the lunchroom harassment was hard to ignore. It was a bitter lesson to learn, but one that has helped him more accurately distinguish a real friend.

We don't want our children to know the sting of rejection, but they probably will. At some point, they are likely to become aware that they are excluded or bullied. When this happens, it's important to keep your response honest, but not overly emotional. It is natural to have very strong emotions when this happens to your child. Parents can process their own emotions with other adults so that they don't inadvertently incite panic in their child as he analyzes the situation. By validating your child's experience, providing honest information and taking care of your own emotions, you help your child through a painful incident.

## Finding friends
### When parents feel unsure socially

Let's rejoin Scott at the topic night on friendship. He continued with his concerns.

"I'm not very social and so I don't know how to help Michael be social," he said. "I can't help him with this because I still don't know how to do this for myself."

Often, parents don't have many social connections or practice with developing new friendships themselves, so they aren't comfortable reaching out to other families. What can you do when you aren't sure which child might be a good match or you aren't comfortable initiating social interactions?

- *Ask teachers*: Teachers interact with our children everyday and know which kids might be good friends for your child. They can be a worthwhile source for finding friends at school.

- *Ask social skills group leaders*: If your child attends a group, ask if the children can exchange contact information in order to get together outside of the group.

- *Ask organization leaders*: If your child regularly attends any community activities (cultural, religious, special interest), ask those leaders if they can suggest possible connections.

- *Reach out to other families*: When you meet other families whose children might be a potential fit, exchange contact information and follow up to make plans for a short, structured family activity.

### Shared interests

One of the best ways to connect kids is through shared interests. My kids have tried a variety of activities. Team sports rarely worked for us. My kids would be out on the field, but they'd be the kids facing the wrong way, trying to hold an in-depth conversation about Pokémon or video games while running down the soccer field. If there were kids they liked on the team, they might enjoy participating, but as the skill level increased and the competition kicked into high gear, my kids chose to leave team sports behind for other pursuits.

Some families have found that groups that focus on interests and activities that aren't sports related or competitive can be a good fit.

Potential community activities to consider:

- *Religious affiliations*: If your family is involved with a religious group/organization, work with them to see how they can support your child's involvement in the educational, social, and cultural events of the community.

- *Musical groups*: If your children enjoy music, there are many outlets for choral and instrumental enthusiasts. Research what's available in your area.

- *Meet-ups*: Online "meet-up" groups are popping up on every conceivable topic and geographic area. If your child has an interest and you can't find a group that exists, think about starting one.

- *Nature groups*: If your child is interested in outdoor activities, finding a group that hikes or camps may work.

- *Individual sports (with a group)*: If team sports aren't your child's thing, sometimes an individual sport that occurs with a group of people is a better option. Fencing, martial arts, or yoga might be possibilities.

For us, making these community activities work required some planning on our part. We always filled out the forms, disclosing what were potential pitfalls (working in a group), and offered a "helpful hints" sheet (see Chapter 3 for an example) so that the leaders would know from day one how to respond to increase the likelihood of successful interactions.

Many successful friendships have blossomed through shared interests and activities—some structured, others not. My sons participated in clubs at school with other kids interested in the same topic. If your school doesn't have any clubs, find a teacher who is willing to support the club and start attracting kids who have shared interests with your own children. Getting involved with clubs and teams at school not only puts our kids in the same room with others with related interests, but also has the added benefit of connecting our kids to their schools and helping them develop a sense of belonging.

## Defining friendship
### Hidden curriculum of friendship
Before you do any of the work of connecting kids to each other, you have to make sure that your kids see the purpose and benefit of playing or being with others. They have to learn what Brenda Smith Myles calls the "hidden curriculum," which includes the information that most people learn implicitly (Myles *et al.* 2004). The problem is that our kids don't "intuit" much and so if we don't explicitly teach the "core competencies" of friendship, they are left behind while other children connect.

We have to check in with our kids and see if they really understand the "purpose of play." Initially they might look at playing with someone as a way to have another person do what they want. They could see having a friend over as a way to have another person around to play their pretend game with a thousand rules. Or they might imagine they'll have someone who will listen to their monologue about a special interest without requesting a change in topic. Play can certainly be a chance for kids who have the same interests to find each other and enjoy exploring them together. In fact, it's one of the best ways for them to interact positively.

At a recent topic night on friendship, Pete, the parent of an 8-year-old boy, was worn out.

"When my child has a friend over, I end up talking to or entertaining the friend while my son goes off and does whatever he wants because he's bored. If I try and bring Tom back in the same room, he'll just bring a book to read and sit near his friend reading. The kids who come over don't know what to do about that. Sometimes they ask to go home. What am I supposed to do?"

Tom doesn't realize that when he has a friend over at his house, his friend will expect to play together. It sounds as if he loses his stamina for interaction. He might be fine for 30 minutes, but a two-hour get together might be too much to expect.

How to help our children understand the hidden curriculum of playing with friends:

- *Social Stories™*: Carol Gray's Social Stories™ can help our children understand the purpose of play and what to anticipate when they host or go to another child's home (Gray 2010).

- *Think out loud*: Be explicit and clear about your expectations for friends coming over or going to someone else's home. Talk about your own experience of feeling like a get-together has gone on too long and how you handled it. Providing language about how to end playing with a friend is important.

- *Plan and structure the time*: I used to set a schedule to help my own children and their friends know how they were going to spend their time. It helped my kids understand how much time would be spent on each activity. It also gave them a chance to practice being flexible as they might decide they wanted to spend more time on one activity and less on another. The key was that the friends had to agree on how to use their time together. At the bottom of any schedule we developed, I would write, "This schedule is subject to change."

- *Short and successful*: Have a short get-together to start. Instead of having a two-hour session at our home, I might offer to take the kids to the park after school or out for ice cream and then bring everyone back to their own home. Build your child's tolerance and ability to be social for longer periods of time. For many years, my oldest son would tell his friends he needed some time to himself and would go home or ask his friend to leave.

Even after practicing the relevant skills needed to interact with peers, it can be confusing to decipher the friendship code. Children and adults may say things they don't mean. People can appear to be friendly but have malicious intent. How can we help our children develop an internal barometer—a gut instinct—to help them know when to be wary of an interaction? How do we turn an intuitive process into a systematic one?

### Warning signs of negative relationships

When my oldest son was in elementary school, another boy in his class said he would be his best friend if he pushed another kid at recess and punched him in the stomach. My son was the largest boy in the class and so he looked tough. Noah came home from school and relayed the situation over dinner.

"Tim said he would be my best friend if I punched John at recess. Why would he tell me to do that?" Noah asked.

I held back my initial reaction, which was, "HE DID WHAT?" and asked instead, "What do you think would happen if you punched another child at recess?" I wanted to check Noah's understanding of how his behavior would be seen by the principal.

"I guess I would get in trouble," he said. "But that's not really fair because Tim told me to and so he should be the one who gets in trouble not me. It's not my fault if he told me to do it."

"I'm so glad you are thinking about this," I said. "You are right that you would be held responsible if you hit someone. Even if someone else told you to do it, you will still be the one who gets in trouble. I'm curious, how did you decide not to do what Tim told you to do? I know that might have been confusing."

"You always tell me not to hit people, so I didn't hit John," Noah answered. "But I want Tim to be my friend. I don't understand why he would tell me to do it. Did he know I would get in trouble?"

"You are asking such good questions," I told him. "Sometimes people we think of as friends say or do things that can hurt us or get us in trouble. It can be hard to tell if someone is a real friend, or is just being friendly in order to get us to do something they want."

"But Tim says he is my friend," Noah said. "If he's my friend, he wouldn't want to get me in trouble."

"I know it is puzzling when people say one thing, but their intention is different from the words they use," I replied. "This is confusing and frustrating for most people. We like people to mean what they say. I think it might help if we make a chart with examples of how a real friend will behave. Let's try to do it together for a few minutes."

**Table 4.1**: Characteristics of a friend

| A friend will... | A friend will not... |
|---|---|
| Be nice to you | Tell you to hurt other people |
| Like you for who you are | Tell you to hurt yourself |
| Share interests | Make fun of you |
| Be silly with you | Bully or harass you |
| Do friendly teasing | Make you feel bad about yourself |
| Take turns doing what each of you likes | Only think about themselves |
| Think about your feelings and interests | Take advantage of you |

Seeing the characteristics of a friend (Table 4.1) in black and white helped Noah articulate what had been baffling and uncomfortable. My son had never realized that someone who said they were his friend might be manipulating or bullying him. Once we made the chart, we used it to think through other situations when Noah was unsure whether another child was being a good friend. The chart also helped Noah understand that if he wanted to be seen as someone else's friend, these were also the qualities he would need to show.

## Hidden curriculum of making plans
Seeing our children yearn for a friendship but not be able to have it feels like getting punched in the gut. I remember when Noah

was in early elementary school and wanted one boy in his class to come over. We were still at the stage where parents call each other to make plans for their children. Noah was glued to my hip as I made the call. "Hi, this is Brenda Dater calling, Noah's mom. He'd like to know if Nick could come over to play this weekend."

Silence on the other end of the line. That was never a good sign.

"I'm sorry, he's busy this weekend," Nick's mom answered. "Maybe another time."

No mention of how nice it was of us to call or when a good time might be. Another bad omen. Noah couldn't understand why this was a bad weekend.

"What's he doing?" Noah asked. "When can he play? Maybe we should go over and ask him? Maybe his mom didn't understand that we could play anytime this weekend."

The questions would continue unabated and then the meltdown would come.

"When are you going to call him again? You have to call him again. Call right now!"

"We can't call right now honey," I said. "We just called two minutes ago. We can call another friend. But Nick's mom said they were busy this weekend, so when a parent says their child is busy for the whole weekend, that means you can't call back and ask again until the weekend is over. Otherwise it looks like you're bothering them, even though all you want to do is play with your friend. We can call a different friend or we can find something else to do. Which will you pick?"

When our kids have an idea in their head of what they want to do, no other plan can seep in. They haven't developed problem solving skills that allow them to handle the glitches that occur when trying to make plans with people. We need to help them shift from the unsuccessful plan to another option. We do this by explaining the process for making plans with friends.

Sometimes our kids need more than verbal reminders to help them understand the hidden rules about making plans. Using a visual tool, like Table 4.2, helps our kids process information more effectively. A conversation may seem as if it's getting the information from your brain into theirs, but often it doesn't change how they feel or what they do. When we use a visual aid, it helps slow down the conversation, eases our own frustration, and can help them see the process for solving problems.

Kids with AS have a hard time with internal self-talk—what we tell ourselves when something doesn't go our way. The self-talk they do use tends to be negative, "that will never work," or "I can't do it." We need to give them some options for how to frame their thinking when they have to switch their plans; it helps them avoid perseverating on negative thoughts and feelings.

**Table 4.2**: Making plans: problem solving and internal self-talk

| What I want to do: play with Nick | | |
|---|---|---|
| If... | Then... | Internal self-talk |
| Nick is available and wants to play (and, for younger kids, the parents want him to play) | Set a time and place to play | My friend wants to play with me too! |
| Nick isn't available, but wants to play another time | Set a time and place for a different day or call back to set this up for a different day | My friend's just busy right now and that's okay. We'll play another day. |
| Nick doesn't want to play (or his parents don't want him to play) | Stop calling and asking him to play, or pick a different friend to ask, or do something else that I enjoy | He doesn't really want to play with me. I don't like it, but I will find someone who does want to play with me or do something I like. |

For years my son would have difficulty with the notion that you just can't keep calling people and asking them to play. We had to make a visual aid so that he could understand the reasoning. If he called a friend and left a voicemail, he would want to call back every 30 minutes. He would often say that he knows the family doesn't check their messages and so we need to call them back.

Lynne Mitchell, an educational consultant in Massachusetts, talks about the "Rule of three." Someone can say "no" to doing something with you legitimately three times. After that, you have to assume they are not interested and need to stop asking. Likewise, if you say "no" to someone three times in a row, they will assume you aren't interested either. In our family, we had to set a rule that if you leave a message, you have to wait until the next day to call back again and you couldn't call more than two times in one week. Noah would get stuck with his plan for playing with a particular person in a particular way, and he couldn't let go of the idea and enjoy some other person or activity. We had to teach him the difference between showing interest and being annoyingly persistent. Table 4.3 illustrates how much is too much when you are trying to make plans with someone.

**Table 4.3**: Making plans: how much is too much?

| How many times can I ask someone to play/hang out? | | |
|---|---|---|
| **If…** | **Then…** | **Because…** |
| I leave a voicemail | I need to wait until my friend calls or until the next day before I call again | Leaving only one message a day is best because the person will check messages when they are able and call back when they can. If they don't call back, it might be because they don't want to and so if I keep calling, I will be annoying them, which doesn't help make friends. |
| I ask in person | I can ask one time, while we are together | Other people can feel irritated if I keep asking them why they can't play or when we can play. If I just ask one time, it helps them feel positive about me. |
| I ask a few times on different days and the person keeps saying no | I need to stop asking and find someone else to ask or find another activity I enjoy | If someone says they are busy more than three times, it means that they don't want to. If I keep asking, they will get exasperated and might say something mean to me. This is not a good choice for me. |

## How Asperger's can have an impact on making friends

Once our children are aware of the pieces that complete the friendship puzzle, they may struggle to start friendships and help them grow. What seems to get in the way?

### Emotional regulation

Julia, mom of a 9-year-old daughter, spoke up at the topic night on friendship.

"I'm worried about letting my child go over to anyone else's house. What if she has a meltdown or insists on having things her way?" she asked. "Claire throws a fit over every little thing and she hates changes. If I promise something I have to do it. If I try and change it, even if I warn her, she goes into full-blown meltdown. I just don't know how she'll ever manage outside of our house."

Julia is voicing a common concern among our parents. When your child struggles to manage big emotions, it's a challenge to feel comfortable sending her to someone else's home. It's hard to relax if you are wondering how the play date is going from moment to moment. Although all kids can get frustrated with each other, ours tend to have larger and more frequent bursts of emotion that seems out of proportion to the situation. Until Claire can find ways to manage her response to change, through coping and self-calming strategies, it will be hard for her to negotiate the territory of play dates away from home.

How can we help our children to become more emotionally regulated?

- *Teach and practice self-calming techniques*: Each child is unique. No one technique will work for everyone. Here are a variety of ideas that may be worth trying with your own children.

- *Mindfulness meditation*: Breathing, visualization, and muscle relaxation are very helpful for some kids.

- *Deep breathing*: Our kids can be taught how to use deep breathing to stay calm.

- *Listening to music*: Your child can use headphones to listen to an iPod or other portable music player.

- *Reading*: If your child likes to read, this may work well.

- *Emotional support animal*: Many of our kids feel much calmer when they spend time with a family pet. My boys will often cuddle up with our dog when they need extra comfort.

- *Physical comfort*: Some kids like to sit near a trusted adult or get a hug. Others like to wear certain clothes. Many kids like to sit in beanbag chairs.

- *Physical activity*: Some kids like sensory activities like swinging or jumping on a trampoline. Others like walking or yoga.

- *Distraction or time alone with a special interest*: Always a good choice for calming down.

- *Pacing*: Some of our kids need to move their bodies to relieve stress. Don't make them sit when anxious.

- *Consider cognitive approaches*: Our children struggle to understand their own emotions. They often experience life at the emotional extremes and haven't yet learned how to downshift from feeling as if all unpleasant or frustrating experiences are catastrophes. It's very helpful to choose an approach to help children learn about their own emotions and the emotions of others and how they can manage the overwhelming feelings they may experience. Some parents like to enlist the help of a skilled therapist to help guide their child and family through this process. The following books also offer information and direction to help your child put his emotional triggers and reactions in perspective:

- *The Incredible 5-Point Scale* (Buron and Curtis 2003)

- *Asperger Syndrome and Difficult Moments: Practical Solutions for Tantrums, Rage, and Meltdowns* (Myles and Southwick 2005)

- *When My Worries Get Too Big: A Relaxation Book for Children Who Live with Anxiety* (Buron 2006)

- *What to Do When Your Temper Flares: A Kid's Guide to Overcoming Problems with Anger* (Huebner 2008)

- *What to Do When You Worry Too Much: A Kid's Guide to Overcoming Anxiety* (Huebner 2006)

- *My Book Full of Feelings* (Jaffe and Gardner 2006)

- *Exploring Feelings: Cognitive Behaviour Therapy to Manage Anxiety* (Attwood 2004)

## HOW CAN WE HELP OUR CHILDREN MANAGE THEIR EMOTIONS AT A FRIEND'S HOME?

- *Review a key strategy*: Before your child heads off to another child's home, make sure he has one or two calming down strategies that work for him if he starts to feel frustrated. Have your child tell you what he will do if he starts to feel anxious or annoyed.

- *Exit strategy*: It's important for our kids to know they can leave a friend's house if they are feeling overwhelmed. Make sure they know how to tell the family that they need to leave and that they inform you as well.

- *Share relevant information*: It is useful to have a couple of helpful hints to share with a parent who is hosting your child. You don't have to share a diagnosis, as that might not be meaningful to the other parent. But it can be helpful to say, "Claire has a hard time shifting from one activity to the next without a warning. Could you please tell her if you are going to have the kids do more than one thing while they're together. Sometimes I even write it down so that she can see it. Thanks for your help."

- *Role-play*: Practicing how to respond to common situations can help a child feel more comfortable.

- *Social stories™*: These can help your child understand and become familiar with the important aspects of playing with others (Gray 2010).

- *Self-talk*: Teaching some positive self-talk that your child can use when they are feeling unsettled can be helpful. You can teach children to say something positive to themselves when they feel stressed, "Even though this isn't my first choice, I can try it because my friend likes it."

- *Self-advocate*: Some situations are hard to navigate and require adult assistance. Teaching our kids how to ask for support from adults is important. Before your child goes to a new friend's home, you can help her imagine the types of situations that might be challenging and then practice how to seek out help.

- *Choose wisely*: Some parents are more helpful and willing to do the extra work required to help your child manage in a new situation. I sought out parents who I thought would be a good fit (in addition to their child being a good fit). When parents were negative or didn't seem capable of providing the structure or support, I tried to find others or I offered to have the children at my home.

Once our kids learn some emotional regulation skills, they are much more capable of interacting with other people, because the day-to-day glitches that occur for all kids don't set them off as much as they used to. It takes trial and error to figure out which homes are good choices for learning how to play.

## Perspective taking

Our children falter socially because they don't have a good sense of how to connect to other children. Their attempts to join in often seem stilted. They may launch into monologues about their special interest, an interesting fact, or trivia. This can result in confused looks and lost opportunities. I found it telling when I would ask my son, "What does your friend like to do?" His answer was often, "I don't know."

HOW DO WE HELP OUR CHILDREN CONNECT TO THEIR PEERS?

- *Friend files*: Michelle Garcia Winner talks about the friend files we create in our brain to store the important information we learn about other people. Our kids often don't realize that people give us information about themselves through what they say, what they do, and how they look. Cueing our children to use their friend files helps them connect with others (Winner 2000).

- *Observe*: Our children don't tend to be natural observers of social interaction. They miss critical social information that would help them understand how to initiate or join in play with other children. Drawing their attention to how other children play together can help raise their awareness of the steps involved.

- *Think out loud*: Let your child know what you are learning about people and how you figured it out. Make it a part of your everyday conversation so that your internal thought processes become explicit. Just as we share information with our youngest children about safety and explain the rules to them, we need to share the rules for friendship and how we learn about others in a more explicit manner.

- *Structured groups or planned activities*: When you don't know much about someone else, it can be easier to interact this way. Talk with the group leader about expanding opportunities for playing together outside of the group. For children who are a good match, make sure they exchange contact information and practice talking to each other outside of the group time.

## Social pragmatics

Let's rejoin our topic night on friendship to hear what Bella, mom of 10-year-old Anthony, shared.

"When the neighborhood kids are playing outside, he stands on the front lawn and talks at them. They roll their eyes and move farther down the street. Sometimes he chases after them and they keep running away from him. It's so depressing to watch. How do I keep him inside or get them to play with him?"

Bella has two major factors to contend with. First, the children may not be the best choice for Anthony. They continually run away from him, so he doesn't have a willing partner. Second, Anthony's social pragmatic skills are delayed. He doesn't realize how he needs to communicate with these (or other) children. He has not yet figured out that talking at people about your own interests doesn't tend to make them want to be with you. He also doesn't understand or pay attention to the nonverbal communication others send.

### HOW CAN WE HELP OUR CHILDREN USE SOCIAL PRAGMATICS EFFECTIVELY?

- *Focus on nonverbal communication*: "Generally 20–40% of our message is communicated by the words spoken, and the other 60–80% is communicated by what we do while speaking" (Winner 2000, p.94). When I shared this statistic with Noah before he was aware of nonverbal communication, he didn't believe me. He couldn't fathom that tone of voice, gestures, body position, and facial expressions—like smiling or eye rolling—made any difference to the communicative messages we send or receive. To him, the actual words were the only part of the message that merited his attention. Without an understanding of the importance of nonverbal communication, our kids miss 60–80% of the meaning. We need to make sure our children understand nonverbal communication exists and have the opportunity to practice observing and using it in a variety of situations.

- *Video review*: Kids' shows provide opportunities to discuss social pragmatics. Whether animated or live action, choose age-appropriate shows and try pausing the show and talking about social pragmatics—especially nonverbal communication—that you see. Don't overdo this approach; it can take all the fun out of the show if you use it too frequently.

- *Preview, cue and review*: Real-time social situations are much more demanding than slowed-down social teaching in a small group setting. It helps to preview before a real-time event, provide cueing in the moment if possible, and review what worked and what was challenging after the fact.

- *Use visuals to process social situations*: You can use visual tools to "deconstruct" social interactions so that your child can learn from his experiences. Our children can seem as if they understand a dialogue, but often discussion alone doesn't change behavior. Processing more complex social information often requires visual aids to slow down the conversation and allow learning to occur. I particularly like using "Social Autopsies" (Lavoie 2005) and *Social Behavior Mapping* (Winner 2007). These approaches break down social interactions to help children understand how their behavior might be interpreted and responded to by others.

- *Practice in everyday settings*: Our children need to practice these skills out in the real world, which means outside of the social skills group session. You can practice these skills when other kids come to your home. You can also practice these skills out in the community doing activities like eating out, going to a movie, or meeting up with others at a school event.

- *Observe*: Children are sometimes taught scripts or given language for playing with others that doesn't reflect how children in our neighborhoods or schools talk to each other. Have your child observe how children talk to each other during lunch, at recess, and out in the community. You can make a dictionary of common phrases and words, explaining what they mean and when they are likely to be used.

- *Practice with a good match*: It's hard to use social pragmatics effectively in dynamic situations. Be patient and try to find another child who will be a good fit.

## Social appetite and balancing social demands

At a recent topic night, Beth wondered how much she should push her 12-year-old daughter to interact with other children.

"My daughter just wants to be left alone," Beth began. "I know she needs a lot of time to herself. She always has. But how much is too much? It's like pulling teeth to get her to make plans or agree to go anywhere. I don't know when to push and when to back off." How can Beth find the right balance between allowing her daughter the alone time she prefers, yet still help her develop her ability to interact with others?

Many parents ask this same question. All of us have different levels of interest and need for social interaction. We also have different levels of ability and feelings about whether we want to be with other people. We don't want to make value judgments about what the "right" amount of social interaction is for any given person. When social interactions are a lot of work and may not be providing positive feedback, they tend to drain energy and resources and leave us feeling depleted. Just as we need to work slowly and systematically to build physical stamina, we need to offer opportunities to learn and practice the skills required for developing social stamina.

INDICATORS TO HELP YOU FIND THE RIGHT BALANCE
FOR TIME ALONE AND TIME WITH OTHERS

- *Determine ability*: Sometimes parents or teachers will say that a child is choosing time alone over time with others because they prefer it. That may be true, but check what social challenges might be getting in the way of their ability and willingness to seek out and respond to social overtures. It's not a choice if the skill doesn't exist.

- *Social diet*: Just as we try to make sure our children get a mix of activities or ingredients that help them develop physically, we want to build in the right mix of social interactions so that they gain exposure and practice interacting with others. Start from where your child is currently comfortable and slowly expand social opportunities.

- *Allow time for special interests and time alone*: Our children need time away from the constant onslaught of bewildering and anxiety-provoking social situations. Don't take away time alone or special interests as a consequence or punishment. Do build in other activities to supplement and expand their engagement in the larger social world.

## Setting panic aside

Friendship can be a difficult proposition for our children. As they learn how to be a good friend and what to look for in potential friends, my hope is that they will connect with others who share their passions and like them for who they are. As parents, we can provide support, guidance, and practical opportunities to help them discover what friendship has to offer.

# CHAPTER 5

# Homework

*Why is it Hard and What Will Help?*

Why is homework so challenging for our children? They throw fits over work that seems easy and within their capabilities. They refuse help even though they are struggling. They rush through assignments, resulting in a work product below their capabilities, or are unable to finish because they want it to be perfect. Does homework have to be this hard?

Teachers assign homework for a variety of reasons, including reinforcing material taught at school, developing and demonstrating an understanding or proficiency, bolstering study skills or providing time to work on group projects or independent study. They don't intend for homework to be a source of meltdowns, anxiety, or arguments. And yet for many children and families, homework generates significant stress.

In order for our children to reap the benefits from homework, they need to understand what's expected of them, have sufficient supports to do the work required, and have a method for managing problems that arise. As a parent or teacher, it is easy to get pulled off track if a child's behavior appears manipulative. Throughout this chapter you will see that there are a multitude of factors that make homework more challenging for a child with Asperger's, along with ideas for how to minimize the stress, frustration, or anxiety our children experience as a result of it.

Throughout this chapter on homework, you will learn about:

- why homework is hard and what to do to help:
  - the role of executive functioning in homework
  - practical strategies to address common homework challenges:
    - » recording assignments
    - » turning homework in
    - » managing time
    - » planning for long-term assignments
    - » procrastinating—starting and finishing work
- why assignments are confusing and how to make them more clear:
  - understanding what's expected from an assignment and how to do the work
  - practical strategies for school
  - understanding teacher expectations
- parents' role in homework:
  - communicating with teachers
  - offering just the right amount of support.

## Why homework is hard

Dale came to our topic night on homework completely exasperated by his 11-year-old's inability to bring home what he needs to do his work or remember what work needs to get done.

"It's so maddening," Dale explained. "Nick has an assignment book, but he doesn't write in it because he thinks he will remember once he's home. The few times he does write the assignments down, he doesn't bring the right folder or book home so he can't complete the work. On the very rare occasion he does actually complete the assignment, he forgets to turn it in once he's at school. And to top it all off, he blames us when the teacher is upset with him about homework. We don't know what to do anymore."

Why is Nick struggling?

### The role of executive functioning in homework

In their book, *Smart but Scattered*, Dawson and Guare define executive functioning as "the collection of brain-based skills that are required for humans to execute, or perform tasks" (Dawson and Guare 2009, p.13). Because our children's executive functioning skills are delayed, it will take them longer to learn and be able to use them independently. One of the main reasons homework is challenging is because it requires well-developed executive functioning skills.

It's arduous to complete complex tasks when your brain's executive functioning skills aren't fully functional. Our children might not think before they act. They might struggle to manage their emotions when they are frustrated. Our children may find it hard to pay attention to tasks when distractions, fatigue, or boredom set in. Sometimes they procrastinate for extended periods of time and can't seem to start their work. Our kids might appear confused or frustrated because they are unsure how to plan and prioritize. They often seem disorganized. Our children might have difficulty estimating and allocating time effectively. And our kids might not be able to adapt to changes in routine, especially when they feel anxious or stressed (Dawson and Guare 2009).

Our children can have difficulty with any of the components of homework—recording the assignment, bringing home the materials needed, understanding the purpose of the assignment, allocating enough time to do the work, starting the work, ignoring distractions, persisting even when bored or challenged, problem solving when glitches arise, staying calm when frustrated or confused, finishing the work, putting the work away, bringing it back to school, and turning it in to the teacher. Let's start by considering why they struggle with recording and turning in their work and how to help them become more capable and consistent.

## Why recording assignments and turning them in is challenging
### RECORDING ASSIGNMENTS

- *Handwriting*: Many of our children have significant difficulties with fine motor control. Putting pencil to paper requires great effort. Our children may not have the stamina to pay attention to the assigned homework *and* write it down in an assignment book.

- *Verbal directions*: Some teachers mention homework, but don't write it down. For many of our children, verbal directions, unaccompanied by written directions won't be sufficient.

- *Distractions*: Classrooms are busy places and our child's attention may be drawn in many different directions. She may miss the important information the teacher expects her to glean from conversation because she is focused elsewhere.

- *Time pressures*: Usually teachers assign work at the end of the class or day. Many of our children take longer to pack up their bag and walk through the hall. They might feel time pressure as the bell rings and skip the laborious step of writing homework in their assignment book so that they don't miss a bus.

### TURNING WORK IN

- *Inconsistent expectations*: If a teacher collects homework either inconsistently or in multiple ways, it will be harder for our children to understand what they are supposed to do.

- *Organization*: If our children don't know where to keep their homework once they finish it, it often gets left behind.

- *Cues*: If the teacher isn't consistent and there isn't a verbal or visual reminder from her that explicitly states, "I'm collecting homework now!" our children might miss the opportunity to pull their work out of the backpack and turn it in.

## Practical strategies to help children record and turn in assignments
### RECORDING ASSIGNMENTS

- *Recording starts at school*: Work with your child's teacher or team to learn more about how they expect her to track information and how they can help.

- *Be explicit*: Teachers cannot assume that students with Asperger's will implicitly understand an assignment or be able to assess the relevancy of verbal information. Be clear and explicit when assigning work. It can help to preface verbal instruction with, "this is important," to help students focus on critical information.

- *Provide visual cues*: Provide a consistent visual cue, for example writing the assignments in the same place each day, to clarify assignments and due dates.

- *Provide adequate time to record*: Often teachers are giving out the assignment as the bell rings and students are heading out the door. Allow adequate time for the student to capture the information.

- *Utilize assistive technology*: For students with handwriting challenges, the tracking task becomes doubly difficult, as they have to master the information *and* the pencil to paper process. Consider the use of assistive technology to capture and record assignments. Electronic calendars, voice recordings, apps, or templates in a word processing program are potential options.

- *Put homework on a website*: Teach your child to access the teacher's website (if it exists) to check for homework.

- *Tracking templates*: The sample homework template in Table 5.1 provides a way for students to record the assignment, include what materials are needed, estimate amount of time required, and check off work when it's done.

**Table 5.1**: Sample homework template

| Assignment and start date | Materials needed | Estimated and actual time needed | Due date | Check off when turned in |
|---|---|---|---|---|
|  |  |  |  |  |
|  |  |  |  |  |
|  |  |  |  |  |

- *Tracking long-term assignments*: Long-term and multi-step assignments pose additional challenges to executive functioning. If they are tracked on the original day, but aren't included in subsequent days, our children may forget to keep working on them until the deadline slaps them in the face. In addition to recording the type of assignment, they have to break down the individual tasks that need to be completed. Often, our children don't imagine the required steps that inevitably lead to problems completing the project. (See Table 5.4 for an example of a long-term assignment template).

TURNING WORK IN

- Teachers can help by doing the following:

  ○ *Provide a homework bin*: All homework is turned in at the same time and place each day.

  ○ *Provide visual and verbal reminders*: This helps students remember to turn in their work before leaving the classroom.

  ○ *Label folders*: Some students find it helpful to have "homework to do" labeled in one folder (or side of folder) and one folder labeled, "homework to turn in."

  ○ *Weekly folder purge*: In order to keep binders and folders from becoming unwieldy, teachers can set aside time each week for students to sort through errant papers. Teachers can provide models and guidance to clarify which papers need to be kept or discarded.

  ○ *Check out*: Checking out with a teacher at the end of the day helps to make sure the student has captured the homework and has turned in any work due that day.

- Parents can help by doing the following:

  ○ *Refer to the homework template/assignment book*: Have your child practice using the template as a reminder at school. He can't "check off" the assignment on his template until he has turned it in.

  ○ *Provide an organized space for school items*: Have your child choose (with your support if needed) one place to keep all of her supplies and homework. It's much easier for your child to find what she needs when she knows where to keep and look for her schoolwork.

  ○ *Pack up backpacks in the evening*: Try to establish a routine to have your child pack his backpack in the evening for the next school day. Morning time is usually too rushed and papers and books can be left behind.

o *Use a checklist*: Some children like using checklists to mark off when they complete each step. You can create a "turning in homework" routine that includes the steps he needs to do (put homework in folder at home, look in folder when I get to school, give homework to teacher, check off that homework was turned in).

o *Use reminders*: Most children need some type of reminder to turn in their work. Some like post-it notes on folders or binders. Others use electronic reminders.

o *Make homework easily accessible*: Sometimes the systems our children use to organize their homework make it almost impossible for them to find it again. It takes trial and error to find an organizational system that works. Some children like to use one folder for all their homework to turn in. Some have a homework section in a binder. The most important thing is that your child knows where to find his work when it's needed and that the system can be maintained.

### Managing time

Let's revisit our parent topic night on homework. Jerry, dad of 13-year-old Justin, is frustrated by how much time he and his son argue about when to do homework and how long it should take.

"Justin procrastinates big time and then he gets really wound up because he hasn't done the work and it's bedtime," Jerry said. "Here's what happened yesterday after school."

"Hey Justin, how much homework do you have?" Jerry asked after Justin was settled comfortably on the sofa with a snack and a handheld electronic device.

"Not too much," Justin mumbled. "I can do it later."

"How much is not too much?" Jerry asked. "Remember you have a doctor's appointment later."

Justin screamed, "Why didn't you tell me I have something today? Now I'll never get my work done. What's the point of even starting it?"

"Justin, you have lots of time to do your work," Jerry responded. "You have until we go to the appointment and afterwards. How much time do you need to do it?"

"I don't know," Justin fumed. "It doesn't matter. I can't get it done if I have a doctor's appointment."

"Justin, stop playing games now and just start your homework," Jerry replied in a stern voice. "You can get some of it done before we go."

"No," Justin said. "I don't do homework right after school. I always have free time until 4:30 and then I start my homework."

"Today you need to start it earlier," Jerry explained.

"No," Justin stood his ground. "I never start it earlier. 4:30 is when I start. You have to change the doctor's appointment."

"I can't cancel at the last minute," Jerry replied. "We have to go. Just start your homework earlier so you'll be able to finish before dinner."

"No," Justin said again. "I can't. It's not my fault that you made the appointment at the wrong time. I'm not doing my homework until 4:30."

Jerry continued telling us his story, "By this point we'd probably been arguing for about the amount of time it would've taken Justin to do his homework. It's so frustrating to try to get him to see things from another point of view. He gets so stuck in believing one thing and won't consider other interpretations. Plus, Justin gets really upset and yells at me. The day went from bad to worse. He yelled all the way to the doctor and didn't do his homework. I can't promise him that every day will be the same. How do I help him get out of this rut? I'm tired of him arguing with me over every little thing."

Jerry's brought up a very common problem. Our kids don't naturally anticipate how schedule modifications will impact their ability to get their work done. They often have strong emotional reactions to changes in routine. They also struggle with estimating how much time homework will require and how much time they have in a day to accomplish a variety of school and home responsibilities. So what can we do to help our children learn how to manage time and adapt to schedule changes?

## Practical strategies for time management
### CALENDARS

- *Use a calendar to keep track of all activities and responsibilities*: In addition to telling your child about a change, it can help to include it on an electronic or handwritten calendar.

- *Offer choices within a set structure*: The sample calendar in Table 5.2 provides structure to help our children predict what the day will bring. Offering choices within workable parameters allows your child some control. You might include the following information on calendars.

  - *Regularly scheduled appointments*: Therapist, lessons, activities, practice times, and meals are a few possibilities.

  - *Free time*: Our kids worry about when free time will happen as they see their schedule filling up with responsibilities not of their choosing. Build in free time each day so that your child can see when she will have time to do just what she wants.

  - *Homework*: When children are younger, the amount and type of homework they have is fairly consistent day to day or week to week. As they move into the teen years, homework can vary more in amount and degree of difficulty. Estimate how long the entire amount of work will take and schedule it in.

- *Special events*: Make sure to include upcoming events or appointments and include travel time.

- *Plan for change*: Talk with your child about how schedules change when unforeseen events occur. A parent or child might get sick. An emergency might occur. The weather could produce challenges or delays. Our children sometimes struggle with understanding how a larger event impacts their schedule. It can help to take time to explain how a change in one family member's schedule affects others.

**Table 5.2**: Sample calendar

| Time | Monday | Tuesday | Wednesday | Thursday | Friday |
|------|--------|---------|-----------|----------|--------|
| 3:00 | Free time | Piano lesson | Homework | Karate | Free time |
| 4:00 | Homework | Free time | Social group | Piano practice | Free time |
| 5:00 | Free time | Homework | Free time | Free time | Free time |
| 6:00 | Dinner | Dinner | Piano practice | Dinner | Free time |
| 7:00 | Free time | Free time | Dinner | Homework | Dinner |

Adapt the calendar to fit your needs. You can use shorter or longer blocks of time. You can do this electronically or on a large wipe off board. Try different ways to capture the information to see what works best for you.

LEARNING HOW TO BE EFFICIENT AND FLEXIBLE

Let's revisit the difficulty Jerry is having with Justin. He is trying to tell Justin what to do and expecting him to acquiesce. Our children tend to be more flexible when they feel as if their point of view is understood and that they have a say in how to solve a problem.

When my oldest son was convinced that he didn't need to start his homework before 9:00 at night in middle school, I made an appointment to talk with him.

"Noah, I'm wondering why you aren't doing your homework before dinner anymore." I began cautiously.

"I need more free time," Noah answered. "Middle school is really stressful and I don't want to think about doing any work when I get home. It's not that hard, I can do it right before bed."

"Okay, except you seem to be getting upset right before bed when you are trying to do the work," I said. "I wonder if you wouldn't rather have it done earlier in the day and then you could relax right before bed."

"No," Noah replied. "I don't want to do my homework earlier. It needs to be later. I can do it."

"How about if we try an experiment?" I asked. "For the next two weeks, you do your homework right before bed and let's track how frustrated you feel and the quality of your work based on teacher's comments or grades. If it all goes fine, then switching the time makes sense and I won't say anything else about it. But if the data tell a different story, we need to find an earlier time that works better for you. Are you willing to try this out?"

"I guess," Noah responded.

At the end of the two weeks we had some meaningful data.

"So Noah, more than half the time you spent at least 20 minutes complaining about the amount and type of work you needed to do," I shared. "For the first time this year your teachers are asking you to redo sections on your homework. Is it worth it to do the homework late at night if you end up more frustrated by it and you have to spend more time doing it over?"

"But I don't want to do it earlier," Noah replied.

"I bet you'll be less frustrated if you do it earlier," I said. "Let's check the calendar and see if we can try to find times before your brainpower is depleted for the day. We can try out the new time and see if it works better for you."

"Sure," Noah agreed reluctantly. Instead of telling Noah that his plan to do homework late in the evening wasn't a good one, he learned it by trying it out, without dire consequences, and was able to imagine another way to get his work done.

WHAT HELPS OUR CHILDREN THINK ABOUT HOW TO
USE THEIR TIME FLEXIBLY AND EFFICIENTLY?

- *Validate their concerns*: Our children need to feel understood. We can learn quite a bit about what might be contributing to their inflexible responses when we ask questions and listen to their reasoning.

- *Use data*: Instead of lecturing about the merits of your approach and the deficits in your child's, bring objective information into the discussion. I usually start by saying that, "something isn't working well," and sharing data (grades, teacher comments, amount of time spent being upset over work, frustration with assignments). After sharing the data, I'll say, "Let's work together to see if we can solve this problem."

- *Offer a trial basis*: If we force our children to make a change that seems unreasonable or makes them uncomfortable, they may not have the emotional regulation to manage their frustration. I find that offering to "try" a new approach for a short amount of time usually promotes cooperation.

- *Evaluate usefulness*: Have your child rate the usefulness of his time management approach. If he is frustrated or having to work harder than necessary, he may become more flexible about trying another tactic. Offering to evaluate new techniques may help your child be willing to give them a try.

- *Be adaptable*: Even if you have an idea of how your children should handle a problem, be open to the possibility that they will come up with good solutions on their own. Don't assume that your way is the best way for them.

- *Consider alternate options*: Our children often get stuck in their thinking and can't imagine multiple options for addressing a problem. Table 5.3 helps them understand that there's always more than one way to approach a dilemma. For example, if the problem they are having revolves around running out of time for homework, you could fill in the following chart together.

**Table 5.3**: Problem I need to solve

| Not enough time for homework | | |
|---|---|---|
| **Option number 1** | **Option number 2** | **Option number 3** |
| Start homework right after school | Start homework after I have a short break after school | Keep doing homework right before bed |
| **What might happen if I try this option?** | **What might happen if I try this option?** | **What might happen if I try this option?** |
| I might not be able to concentrate because I need a break before starting my work | I would get home from school and have a snack and do what I want and then start my work when the timer goes off | I get so mad at night. I just want to do what I want. It takes longer to do my work |
| **Will I try this first?** | **Will I try this first?** | **Will I try this first?** |
| No | Yes | No |

WHEN EMOTIONS TAKE OVER

"Molly whines all the time," Lisa explained at our homework topic night. "Whenever she has homework to do, she whines about how long it will take. She spends more time complaining about how long it will take than she does doing the work. I start out being understanding and listening, but then I just get fed up. I mean, it seems like such a stall tactic and I know she can do the work. She is wasting time and wearing me out. How do I get her to do her work without complaining so much?"

The other parents share Lisa's concern as a wave of head nods sweeps across the room. Why do our kids spend so much time upset about the work they have to do? Their outbursts make it almost impossible to get any work done. What can we do to help them?

- *Identify and remove triggers*: Find out what type of work or demand is setting your child on edge. Once you know what is setting off the meltdown you can address the homework trigger in the following ways.

  - *Clarify expectations*: Make all expectations explicit. Don't assume that your child will automatically figure out implied meanings.

  - *Order tasks*: Let your child know that when they finish their work they will get a break or free time. If you threaten to take away an activity they were expecting *unless* they do their work, you may end up making the situation worse.

  - *Provide structure*: Sometimes I use a wipe-off board as a visual aid to help my child see what work he has to do. Some of our kids are very stressed when they look at their planner and need to see it in another format. I like to prioritize the order of the assignments and estimate how much time each might take. This helps a child see how much work they really have.

  - *Break down assignments*: If the work is multi-step or abstract, it may help to list each component that needs to be completed.

  - *Provide a trusted adult*: Sometimes our kids need to talk to an understanding adult when they feel overwhelmed. Instead of punishment or assuming a child is being manipulative to get out of work, provide a safe space and person to talk with your child when they are at school or home.

- *Assess calming and coping strategies*: Because most children with AS have difficulties with emotional regulation, we need to make sure they are actively taught calming and coping strategies to help when they feel stressed by the demands of homework (specific suggestions are included in Chapter 4).

- *Provide whining time*: When my kids were younger, I would set a timer for five minutes before homework started. This was their whining time. They could complain all they wanted, and when the timer ran down, they knew it was time to start the work. It worked for my kids because it used humor to handle a frustrating situation and also allowed them to vent a bit, without getting stuck for an indeterminate amount of time.

- *Help them learn to estimate time*: Figuring out how much time tasks require is challenging. Our children often think an assignment will take much longer than it actually does or they underestimate the time needed for complex or long-term work and end up feeling pressured by deadlines. Your child can learn to estimate time by guessing how long something will take and then use a timer or clock to check accuracy. Record the estimate and actual time required so that they can catch any discrepancies and use the information next time they have similar work to do.

- *Work for short amounts of time*: When our children haven't yet developed the capacity to manage their emotions when frustration overwhelms them, we need to reduce the demands. Shortening the amount of time we expect them to work keeps frustration and stress from building. As our children develop their emotional regulation capabilities, they will be able to tolerate working for longer stretches of time.

- *Build in breaks*: Breaks can help our kids replenish the stamina they need to do their work. One problem our children have with breaks is that they may choose something too intriguing and can't seem to get back to their work. They also take a lot of breaks so that it ends up taking them hours to finish work. We need to help our children find effective breaks.

- *Assess what works*: Once our children know the purpose of a break—to help them get through their work—it's time for them to help figure out what might work well. Start by evaluating the effectiveness of current breaks. Do they provide a renewed sense of concentration or stamina? Can your child transition between work and breaks and back to work without major upset? How much time do they spend working and how much do they spend on break? Once you know which breaks are working and which aren't, you can generate possible options to try.

- *Cue transition back to work*: Even when our children choose a break that isn't too engaging, they might be slow to get back to their homework. For some children, setting a timer for a five-minute break can help cue them when to shift from break to homework. For others the cue might be finishing a snack or a walk around the block.

- *Differentiate between special interests and breaks*: Often our children want to have their special interest be their break from work. The problem is that special interests are notoriously difficult to shift out of after only a short amount of time. Let your child know when she will have more extended time to devote to all-consuming passions and have her focus shorter breaks on relaxing, but not too diverting, activities.

## Planning and managing long-term assignments

Chris came to the parent topic night to try to understand why his 16-year-old son couldn't stay on top of high school projects and papers.

"Whenever Charlie has more than a week to complete a project, he doesn't seem to know how to manage it," Chris explained. "He says he has it under control and that he doesn't need to talk to his teachers. But then the day before it's due, he'll start blaming everyone else for not telling him what he needed to do. He never seems to connect the assignment rubric with the work he needs to do and he seems surprised when he's missing major parts of the paper. He's a smart kid, why does he fall apart with long-term work?"

Frequently, schools and teachers expect students to already have learned how to break down long-term assignments. So what can we do when our children haven't learned how to manage this type of work?

## Practical strategies for managing long-term assignments

- *Explicitly teach steps*: Often our children don't see all the steps required to complete an assignment. When a long-term project is given, it will help tremendously if teachers are able to break down the larger assignment into its individual tasks with students and assign timelines for each task. Making the implied steps explicit helps our children understand what is required and how the completion of each part contributes to the final product.

- *Visually track each step*: The long-term assignment planner in Table 5.4 is an example of a multi-step project tracking system. Sarah Ward, a speech and language pathologist specializing in executive functioning, encourages students to include steps that are expected but not explicitly listed by teachers. For example, students often forget to check that their project adheres to the teacher's written or verbal instructions. Ward also recommends any edits that result from comparing a draft of an assignment to a teacher's rubric be listed as the last step before turning in an assignment. This way our children know that editing is included as part of the project.

**Table 5.4**: Long-term assignment planner

| Assignment and start date | Tasks and materials needed | Estimated and actual time required | Due date | Check off when turned in |
|---|---|---|---|---|
| | | | | |
| | | | | |
| | | | | |

Always work backward from your due date so that you allow enough time to complete all the tasks.

- *Schedule teacher check-ins*: Regularly scheduled teacher check-ins help students stay on task. It helps to have the teacher work directly with the student instead of the parent trying to manage the project.

### Procrastinating—starting and finishing work

Dan, dad of 12-year-old Eli, came to the topic night with questions about his son's ability to concentrate on his work.

"Eli can work for hours on the newest video game," Dan said. "He can spend half a day building Lego creations. He can read Harry Potter all weekend. But he can't seem to pay attention to his work for more than a few minutes at a time. Or, he'll keep saying he's going to start his work, but then three hours will pass and he hasn't even begun. Last night I timed him to see how long he could work before taking a break. He got up to use the bathroom or get a snack or read something online or go outside every four minutes. How can I get him to do his work?" What can parents do when their children seem unable to start or stay focused on their work?

### Practical strategies for starting work and sticking with it

- *Create cues to start work*: Sometimes our kids need a cue that prompts them to think, "I need to start my work now." Check with your child to see which of the following might be worth a try:

- ○ Electronic alert (on phone, computer, tablet, calendar)

- ○ After an event (having a snack, feeding a pet, coming home from school)

- ○ Setting a timer and starting work when it rings

- ○ Verbal reminder from a parent.

- *Use timers*: Verbal reminders aren't usually sufficient to get our children to end a task they like and start one they don't prefer. Timers can help them see how much time they have left or how long they have to work on something less interesting.

- *Consider proximity*: Sometimes our children need us nearby when they start their work. My kids would come into the kitchen while I made dinner or I might sit at the table with them doing my own work while they did theirs.

- *Consider distractions*: Evaluate your child's homework space. Does she have access to other interests that will pull her attention away from her work? Try to keep distracting items away from the homework area. Also consider what other people are doing in the space your child is using for homework. Are other family members on computers or watching television? It will be hard to focus on work if other people are doing distracting activities nearby.

- *Consider time of day*: Many children with Asperger's also have difficulties with attention. It's not that they can't focus at all, but it is harder to focus on something that isn't of great interest. For those children who take medication to help with attention issues, it may help to try to do work before medication wears off. Sometimes older students stay at "homework club" to complete their work before they head home.

- *Consider boredom*: Completing work that is boring takes more effort. Our children need help understanding that sometimes they need to do tasks that aren't particularly interesting. Due to their challenges with perspective taking, they may not realize how other people think about tasks that are boring ("I can get through this and then do something more interesting," or "This won't take too long—I can just do it"). Thinking out loud together about how different people manage their boredom in order to complete a task may help. Some possible incentives that help people manage boring tasks might include:

  ○ listening to music

  ○ building in short breaks

  ○ chewing gum or sour candies to increase alertness

  ○ planing to do a fun or relaxing activity after work is done.

- *Consider challenge*: Just as boring tasks take more effort, challenging assignments also require our children to expend more effort than they might have available. Assignments can be challenging for a variety of reasons, including:

  ○ *Open-ended writing prompts*: Open-ended writing prompts don't provide our children with enough information. They don't know what questions to answer or what is most relevant to write about when faced with an abstract question. Teachers can help by providing questions and models to help our kids structure their writing and understand what information or experiences should be included in their response.

  ○ *Handwriting*: Any writing task can be seen as too challenging because of the effort required for pencil to paper tasks. If your child doesn't have the fine motor coordination to write fluidly, the task becomes onerous regardless of the content of the assignment. Teaching keyboarding or using other assistive technology to help your child "show what he knows" often helps.

○ *Group work*: Understanding what is required when working in a group is often challenging. If other students intuitively understand their roles, how to arrange meetings, and communicate using social media, but your child doesn't, it will be more stressful to manage group work. Your child may end up without any role or with too much of the work at the last moment. Clarifying roles at the beginning of any group project and having teachers assign groups may help.

○ *Drawing or making models*: Any assignment that requires fine motor control will demand more effort from your child if she has these types of challenges. Consider what other ways your child can show what she knows without the pain of putting pencil to paper. Assistive technology software can help with drawing or manipulating shapes. Taking pictures and making a power point presentation can confirm knowledge of art. There is always more than one way to demonstrate proficiency.

○ *Showing your work*: Showing your work is hard because it requires you to understand the perspective of your teacher. It also requires you to think through how you arrived at the answer. For many of our children, they know the answer, but they don't know *how* they know the answer. For my son, his lack of understanding the purpose for showing his work became clear when he came home from elementary school and announced, "My teacher must be really stupid. She wants me to show my work, but if she doesn't understand how to do the problem, then she shouldn't be teaching. I'm not going to do her job for her." Noah's comment made me realize that he had no idea why his teacher would ask him to do this task. I had to explain, "Noah,

I think you are missing information that other students might have. Teachers don't ask you to show your work because they don't know the answer. They ask because they want to understand your thinking process and how you arrived at the answer. This helps them decide if you truly understand the material or if you were just lucky and guessed correctly." Noah still didn't want to show his work, but he didn't feel the great injustice he did earlier when he felt taken advantage of.

- *Consider incentives*: When our children face tasks that require extensive effort, they may need incentives to help them disregard their desire to quit. Incentives help our children persist through tasks that seem either too challenging or aren't to their liking (Dawson and Guare 2009). I know when I have an overwhelming job to do or I have to take care of something I find unappealing, incentives help me stick with it until completion.

## Understanding what's expected from an assignment and how to do the work

When my oldest son was in middle school, one of the assignments he received was to describe one of the conflicts in detail for a literary analysis. He was provided with a full sheet of blank paper to fill. He typed the following as his response, "One of the conflicts is when Mr. White is thinking about what he's going to wish for with the monkey's paw. This is character vs. self-conflict." He turned this in and got an A grade.

I had remembered this assignment because when he'd been working on it at home, I'd asked him, "How long of a response do you think your teacher is expecting?"

"It's fine Mom," Noah responded. "I'm done."

"Noah, look at the directions again and see if you think you've answered everything," I said.

"I did it already," he yelled. "I don't need you to tell me what to do."

I could see this was headed in the wrong direction, but couldn't help myself as I said, "Noah, look at the sheet of paper they gave you to answer the question. It's a full blank sheet— what do you think that means?" I asked.

"It means leave me alone," he replied. It was good to see that his pre-teen sarcasm was developing nicely. It was clear this conversation was pointless and I let it drop. What was making Noah so certain that he was right? Why was he so resistant to checking his work?

## Why do our kids struggle with editing or checking their work after a first draft?

- *Done means done*: When our children feel as if they have finished an assignment, they are none too eager to revisit or discuss any aspect of it with a parent or teacher. From their point of view, they have finished the work and they no longer have to think about it. This is rigid thinking in action, with no room for alternative perspectives.

- *Faulty perspective*: Because our children tend to miss subtle, nonverbal, or implied messages (like a blank sheet of paper suggesting that the student write a full page response) they can easily misunderstand or misinterpret their teacher's expectations. It is very difficult to convince them to reevaluate their inaccurate point of view once it is set.

- *Anxiety*: If our children feel anxious about an assignment, they will appear less flexible. They might be anxious because the assignment is confusing or hard. They might be anxious because past experience with this type of assignment was negative. They might be anxious because they want their work to be "perfect," but can't seem to get it to reflect their vision.

- *Task avoidance*: When our children can't do a task—they are likely to avoid it. Not understanding how to write a longer analysis or finding it too challenging could have contributed to my son's strong reaction.

## Understanding the teacher's point of view

When you have questions about your child's homework or your child seems to be struggling excessively, it's important to talk to his teachers. When I made an appointment with Noah's team and asked about what was expected from a middle school student on this type of assignment, one of the teachers responded, "We know he's in special education, so we take that into account when we grade his work."

"So writing two sentences in response to this question wouldn't be considered 'A' material for a general education student?" I asked.

"No," the teacher responded. "We would expect them to write a full page."

"How is Noah going to learn that you want him to write a full page and what type of information needs to be included in his response if he gets an A for writing two sentences?" I asked, truly curious. I was met with blank stares as everyone looked around the table at each other. "I appreciate that you're trying to be responsive to his writing challenges," I continued. "But instead of just modifying the assignment, could we talk about how he will learn how to write?" The stares around the table continued, with no one answering my question. How do you work with the school when your child seems unaware of the purpose of an assignment and how to complete it?

## Practical strategies for understanding the purpose of an assignment and how to do the work
SUGGESTIONS FOR SCHOOL

- *Actively teach terminology*: Our children don't automatically make abstract concepts concrete. They miss the implied understandings that other students pick up more easily. Teachers need to explain and give examples of the style of writing they expect when they ask students to do any of the following:

- describe in detail

- compare and contrast

- summarize

- explain

- analyze

- infer.

- *Practice if-then problem solving*: Once our children understand the different types of assignments and how to approach them, they can then practice assessing the purpose of new assignments. For example, "If my teacher is asking me to compare and contrast two poems, then I need to make a list of the similarities and differences to start."

- *Directly teach a skill*: Sometimes teachers will say that a student will develop a particular skill—like writing—as they mature. Maturation is helpful, but it alone is not sufficient to help our children learn a skill they are missing. Our children need direct, explicit instruction in order to become competent writers.

- *Provide scaffolding*: Scaffolding is the support we provide while a student is learning a new skill. It might include coaching, models, templates, key questions, or outlines. Teachers need to provide sufficient support for children while they are learning and generalizing skills. We need to provide just enough scaffolding so that the child can be successful (Dawson and Guare 2009). We don't do the work for him *or* expect him to manage without any support while learning a new skill.

- *Provide appropriate accommodations or modifications*: Modifications change what is being taught or expected from students. Accommodations allow students to work around their disability, but they are still expected to know the same material and answer the questions as fully as other students. An accommodation could be allowing a student to use a computer to write their essay instead of having to use a pencil. A modification would be allowing a shorter essay or fewer questions on a test. Both modifications and accommodations are important for our children. It's important to figure out what mix of accommodations or modifications might help our children learn skills. Ask *how* a skill is being taught, especially if the teachers have modified their expectations for what your child can do.

### CLARIFYING TEACHER EXPECTATIONS

- *Explicit verbal and written expectations*: Sometimes teachers assume our children already understand implied information and aren't explicit about their own expectations. Being specific and clear about expectations helps our children. When teachers provide verbal instructions or explanations, it helps if they also offer a written version. It can be challenging to process verbal information quickly enough or to process both verbal and written simultaneously (Attwood 2007).

- *Assignment rubrics*: Rubrics provide a framework to help our children know what they should focus on in an assignment. They give the student parameters for success and clarify necessary components that the student must include.

- *Assignment outlines*: Outlines that explain how and when items need to be completed can be a great help by clarifying student responsibilities and breaking down complex tasks.

- *Problem solving suggestions*: It helps when teachers explain how they want their students to handle problems with work. Otherwise our children can get stuck when problems arise, unsure of how to proceed. Often when confusion sets in, our children will avoid the problem or get very anxious because they don't know what to do. Having teachers explain that questions or confusion are part of the learning process and giving ideas for how to ask for clarification or think a problem through are helpful.

- *Teacher check-ins*: Teacher check-ins help students stay on track. When students are younger these can be built into the beginning and end of the day. As students get older and can advocate more, they can practice scheduling appointments with their teachers to check in regularly.

- *Writing process expectations*: If teachers expect students to know a process for writing that includes brainstorming ideas, planning, writing a draft, editing, receiving feedback, and ensuring the final product includes all the important elements, that process needs to be explained clearly and visually. If the teacher talks about the process at school, but doesn't supply written information to support it, the student may not remember or may not think it's important once they are working at home. Parents cannot usually convince their children to follow a specific process unless the teacher has made the expectation explicit.

## Parent's role in homework

Stan came to the homework topic night amazed at how much work he put into his son's homework.

"Each time Stu has a paper to write, I spend hours sitting with him to encourage him to keep writing," Stan explained. "I edit his papers and make suggestions. But he's 14 years old, when is he going to do this all on his own? I'm guessing his teachers don't want me sitting with him until he's done with his work, but if I get up to do something else, he stops too. I don't think they have any idea how much work I put in so that Stu can write a decent paper. Last time I met with the school, they said how much Stu's writing had improved! They think he's done this all on his own, but I've been working with him for hours each week. Will he ever be able to do this without my help?"

Stan's story is familiar. When our children have a meltdown over unclear assignments, work that is too challenging, or feel unsure about how to get organized, we want to help them handle the situation and lower their anxiety or frustration. Although the intention is noble, the execution may lead to more problems. What can we do instead?

## Practical strategies for providing just the right amount of homework support to your child

- *Talk to the teacher*: Let the teacher know your child's reaction to the assignment. No teacher wants a student to suffer, but they can't help if they don't know. Ask the teacher how much time she expects your child to spend on the assignment. You can send back work with the time marked off showing what your child was able to accomplish in the time frame given.

- *Ask for guidance*: Ask the teacher for suggestions on how to help your child without doing too much. You can also include a note with the assignment explaining what support you provided and what worked so that the teacher can see what type of support helps.

- *Have your child contact the teacher*: Remind your child that sometimes homework is frustrating for all kids and that when kids get stuck, checking in with the teacher can help. Often kids with Asperger's do not want or are unable to ask for help. They feel as if they have failed if their work isn't perfect or they feel like giving up if the work presents too large a challenge. Getting them accustomed to reaching out for information or help to solve academic problems is good practice for life.

- *Don't do their work*: Parents feel unsure about stepping back when their children struggle with work. But teachers and schools have no way of assessing what your child needs if you are doing some of his work for him. It is hard to see your child struggle, and even fail, when it comes to academics, especially when that might be the only area where he shines. Unless you plan on doing his work when he is at college, or going to his place of work to make sure his reports are well written, you need to let schools see what your child can do unassisted by you. It's okay to provide support, but be clear with the teachers about what scaffolding you provide in order to help your child be successful.

- *Shift to school*: When kids consistently struggle with homework and have meltdowns at home over it, it may be time to consider doing the work at school. When children are in middle and high school, they may be able to do their work during "homework club" after school or during free blocks in their schedule. Talk with your team about how to shift homework to school so that your child can get the support she needs to complete her work.

## Setting panic aside

It can be frustrating and distressing to watch our children struggle with homework. We need to keep in mind the challenges our children face when asked to complete tasks that depend on strong executive functioning skills. But with time, instruction, and practice our children can understand which strategies and supports help them manage the demands of homework.

CHAPTER 6 ———————————————————————

# Extended Family and Friends

We all want to feel understood and accepted by our families and friends. But it's easy to feel estranged from them when you have a child on the autism spectrum. We find ourselves having to provide information, clarify behavior, and repair relationships when misunderstandings and social missteps occur because our children react unconventionally. Unsolicited advice can be difficult to hear, especially when we harbor self-doubt about how we interact with our children. Each inquiry and well-intentioned comment can be seen as an assault against our parenting.

Yet we require support when dealing with the inevitable highs and lows of parenting kids with AS. We have to be able to interact with our extended families and friends without raising our blood pressure or increasing feelings of isolation. We need to recognize that our family and friends have issues in their own lives that cause them concern. No one is immune to life's inevitable hardships.

Some extended families are close and support each other. Others might not get along or may feel distant. Some friends may help us feel that we are part of an understanding community, while others increase our sense of being different. Still, we all seek to be understood—we want others to intuitively comprehend what we, and our children, need. But if we don't provide information and guidance, the likelihood of that is slim.

Just as our children need us to understand how they see the world, we need to understand our extended families' and friends' points of view as well. Then we can help them appreciate our perspective and, with patience, we can help our children and families understand and get along with each other.

Throughout this chapter on extended family and friends, you will learn that:

- parents are the interpreters for their children and family:
  - they help extended family members understand the *why* behind the behavior
  - they help their children understand what to expect from different people, settings, and activities
- parents are advocates for their children:
  - they set parameters for successful interactions
  - they clarify what their children need
- parents need to develop realistic expectations for grandparents and other family members:
  - handling emotions when grandparents seem to favor a "typical" grandchild
  - sharing joy and celebrating relatives' accomplishments
- parents need to build their friendship networks:
  - beware of toxic friendships
  - look for reciprocity in friendships.

## Parents as interpreters

At a parent topic night, Joanne described a family dinner with her in-laws that went poorly.

"My kids were hungry and started eating before my mother-in-law, Sally, brought all the food to the table. By the time Sally sat down, Erin, my 8-year-old, was ready to leave and was nearly jumping out of her chair. Thomas, my 10-year-old with Asperger's, wasn't using a fork and knife and was talking with his mouth full of food. He looked like he just smelled a skunk and said, 'What's that awful smell?' That's when my mother-in-law lost it."

"'Thomas,' she yelled in a tone I didn't know she was capable of, 'that's rude. If you can't appreciate the food put in front of you, you need to leave the table now!'"

What was Joanne supposed to do with a hungry child overwhelmed by his sensory sensitivities and an offended mother-in-law?

### Unrealistic expectations and incorrect assumptions

Joanne is expecting everyone in the room to know what she knows and to act accordingly. She's expecting her children to know that when you have a more formal meal with a group you wait until everyone is seated before you start eating. She is also expecting her older child, even though he has Asperger's, to know to use a fork and knife and not to talk when his mouth is full of food. She is expecting that Thomas will be able to contain his displeasure at the noxious (to him) smells during the meal. She is expecting her in-laws to know that younger children need to eat earlier before they get overly hungry and that her son still struggles to use a fork and knife due to his motor-planning challenges. Joanne also hopes her in-laws will demonstrate emotional regulation and be able to decode her son's rude comments for what they illustrate—an overwhelmed sensory system and challenges with impulse control and an inability to take the perspective of others at the table. Lastly, Joanne expects her husband to speak up and support her and their children so that she doesn't have to. She has brought all kinds of expectations to dinner, but they are dining alone.

*Explaining behavior before it occurs*

Once family members understand why certain behaviors occur, they might have more patience and be able to set the stage for success. Joanne can start the conversation by being positive and appreciative. Explaining behavior that appears rude but is fueled by anxiety, social confusion, or frustration may sound like rationalizing. It takes practice and great self-control to keep the conversation focused on your goal—providing an explanation and asking for understanding and support. Before a conversation dive-bombs into an argument about whose child-rearing philosophy is most sound, end it as calmly as you can and take a break. Let's imagine what might happen if Joanne had the following conversation ahead of time.

"Mom, I know you like to have these sit down dinners with all the grandchildren—it's really nice of you to cook a delicious meal for us. I just wanted to share with you that it's hard for Thomas to manage a fork and knife. At home I still have to cut his food for him because he doesn't have good fine motor control, and that means things like using a fork and knife, or tying his shoes, or handwriting are really hard for him. He also forgets to not talk when his mouth is full of food. We're working on these things with him, but it takes a long time and it would be a great help to me if you could ignore him when he shows less than stellar table etiquette. For me, it's a success to see him sitting at the table for more than three minutes."

"You do too much for him," Sally responded. "He'd learn to use a fork and knife if you'd just make him do it himself. That's how I taught my children when they were younger than Thomas."

Joanne needs to be careful at this juncture. She can engage in a debate about why her approach is a better fit for her son, but given Sally's earlier comments, it will not be well received. One of the most challenging parts of emotional conversations is knowing when to quit. Our rational brain might recognize that we should stop talking, but our emotional side is relentless and feels the need to justify and explain repeatedly. For Joanne, finding ways to end a difficult conversation and not feel defeated in the process are important.

"It sounds like we both have different experiences raising our children. You have a wonderful son and so do I—we both must have done something right," Joanne offered with a smile and quickly ended the conversation on a less controversial note. Although this may not be as satisfying as responding with a litany of articles, books, and professionals who support Joanne's perspective, she found a way to acknowledge her mother-in-law's experience without negating her own.

### Responding to behavior after an incident

After these types of exchanges, we need to do repair work between our children and the people who have felt offended or wronged by their interactions. I highly recommend teaching all children, teens, and adults with social communication challenges how to apologize. This isn't because they are always in the wrong, but rather because apologies help others feel better about us when we make a social mistake. First, Joanne needs to explain the situation to Thomas and help him cope with the outburst while getting him some food. As a parent, your first priority is checking in with your child and helping him learn from the experience. How could Joanne have responded quickly and calmly to help her son? How could she have approached the conversation with Sally?

"Thomas, come into the kitchen with me," Joanne said. "Don't worry, you will get to eat."

With this comment, Joanne is letting Thomas know that he doesn't need to be alarmed. She knows his greatest concern is his hunger. She helps him by reassuring him that food will be available. Her focus on his greatest concern (I'm hungry), instead of his grandmother's greatest concern (saying something rude), helps him stay calm. As a "first responder," Joanne cannot concern herself with anyone else's reaction except Thomas's. She helps Thomas remain calm and understand the fast-paced emotional interaction that just occurred.

Once Thomas is reassured, Joanne can have a short conversation with him to help him understand his grandmother's point of view. Joanne knows that Thomas would not want to intentionally upset his grandmother, so she can clearly explain how his words and actions were interpreted.

"I know that you have a very sensitive sense of smell and when you smell certain things, like fish, you feel sick to your stomach."

"Oh, that's what that was," Thomas said. "I thought I was going to be sick."

"Here's what you didn't realize though," Joanne explained. "Grandma spent time making this dinner for us. She gets very upset when people make negative comments about her food. She thinks you're being rude and that you don't care about the time and effort she spent doing a nice thing for you. She over-reacted by yelling at you and telling you that you couldn't eat dinner. She didn't understand your sensitivity and you didn't understand hers."

"But Grandma's a great cook," Thomas said. "I love her food. I just don't like fish."

"So the next time there's a smell at mealtime that makes you feel sick, what could you say instead?" Joanne asked.

"I don't know."

"How about, could you please move the fish to the other end of the table?" Joanne suggested.

"I'll try," Thomas said. "I'm really hungry, can I eat now?"

"One more thing before we sit at the table again," Joanne continued. "You and Grandma both over-reacted. You both need to repair the damage so that you can start to feel better again. Can you think of a way you can make this better for you and Grandma?"

"I could give her a hug," Thomas offered. "But I'm really hungry. I need to eat. Can I hug her tomorrow?"

"It would be great if you could go hug her right now," Joanne said. "It will help her feel better. I'll carry your food for you. Could you try it?"

"I guess," Thomas answered. "Can I eat now?"

Joanne knows that both Thomas and his grandmother like hugs. One of the nice aspects of repairing relationships is that they don't always have to include the word, "I'm sorry." You can get the point across with a hug and a kind word.

Just as our children with social communication challenges need support and understanding and a chance to learn from stressful interactions, our family members need our interpretation skills as well. Joanne might have found a time later in the evening, maybe while cleaning up from dinner, to continue the conversation.

"I can certainly understand how the words and tone Thomas used made you upset," Joanne said. "He still tends to blurt out the first thought that comes into his head. I agree with you that what he said was unacceptable, but I also understand that he said it because he hasn't learned how to manage his strong negative reactions to smells that make him feel sick. We're working on it with him and if our goal is to help him manage these situations and express himself in a more socially acceptable manner, then we need to explicitly and calmly explain the social faux pas and help him think through other possible responses. It's not easy or quick, but it's also not intentional on his part. He adores you and didn't intend to insult you with his comment."

"I don't understand why this is so hard for him," Sally puzzled. "He was so rude tonight. I don't want to make it worse for him. But I don't want him to be allowed to talk that way at the table."

"We all have the same goal," Joanne clarified. "But for Thomas, how he reaches that goal will be different. It takes time problem solving and explaining why other people interpret certain words or actions negatively. If punishing him worked, I would support it. It doesn't and it won't, and so I don't use it for him. I will teach him what he needs to know and we can all support him by helping him remember to 'try again' when he uses words that can be construed as rude. Punishing him for what he hasn't yet been able to master doesn't teach him to do it differently. It confuses and frustrates him, which doesn't lead to behavior change. I can understand your frustration with his behavior. But I hope the explanation helps and that we can work together to support him."

*Helping our children understand what to expect*
*from different people, settings, and activities*

Getting along with people who have different agendas for how we spend time together can be challenging. As much as we work with our extended families to understand our kids, we need to work with our kids to understand their family members and friends too. How can we help our children develop the capacity to be flexible when expectations collide? Let's visit a topic night on extended family and see what Debbie, parent of 14-year-old Duncan and 12-year-old Sean, wanted to share.

"I was so nervous going to my cousin Ted's for a family reunion," Debbie began. "Last time we were all together, Ted yelled at my boys because they wanted to watch YouTube videos. Ted plays every sport imaginable—his garage is a shrine to all things ball related. It's as if my kids are allergic to sports. They don't mind being outside, just don't throw a ball anywhere near them. Ted feels it's his duty to teach my boys how to play a sport and everyone ends up yelling or in tears."

"I've tried to talk to Ted about my boys and their abilities, challenges, and interests, but it doesn't seem to make a difference," Debbie continued. "This time we showed up and Ted was ready with gloves and baseballs and herded us into the backyard before we could take off our jackets."

"Okay boys, pick up the gloves and I'll hit some balls to you," Ted said.

"I don't want to," Duncan responded, "it's boring."

"Not an option buddy," Ted replied, ignoring all the information Debbie had shared with him. "Pick up the glove."

"No way," Duncan said. "This sucks."

"He was done trying before he even started," Debbie explained. "I wish Ted could change how he interacts with my kids, but I've tried for years and nothing changes. How can I help my kids manage being at Ted's without causing more problems?"

Debbie has tried to help her cousin understand her children. Sometimes that information sharing is enough to change the dynamic and make family events more comfortable for all. In this case, Debbie needs to shift her attention to helping her children understand their cousin. Ted seems to be the type of person who believes he knows best what others need. He seems to believe that sports are a panacea for all the social challenges Duncan and Sean share. Ted is well-intentioned but misguided in his approach. He will most likely continue to push his agenda at family gatherings. How can Debbie use these family events as an opportunity for Sean and Duncan to practice understanding other people's points of view?

### HIGHLIGHT HIDDEN SOCIAL INFORMATION

- *Review*: Help your children think through what past interactions have been like. What has worked well with this family member? What has been problematic? Do your children see any patterns?

- *Think out loud*: Clarify the positive intentions of family members. Help your children understand why a family member acts they way they do (if you know!).

- *Problem solve*: Brainstorm different ways your children can interact with family members. Don't assume it will just get better on its own.

For example, Debbie could try the following conversation with Duncan and Sean before going to Ted's next time.

"What do you think Ted will want us to do when we get to his home for the reunion?" Debbie asked.

"I just want to watch some YouTube videos," Sean replied. "I can't play baseball. I hate it. It's stupid."

"Ted likes us all to be together and he thinks kids like to play sports," Debbie explained. "He wants you to be included. He can't imagine that you wouldn't like to play. I wonder if there's a way for you to be outside with everyone without playing the game?"

"I just want to watch videos," Duncan added. "I don't want to talk to anyone. Everyone talks too much. It's annoying and boring."

"You guys are both really good at taking videos," Debbie said. "What if you took videos of other people playing the game and then you could edit it to share with the family? That way you could be outside with everyone and you could do something you like. Do you think we could try that?"

"It's better than getting yelled at," Sean answered. "But I still want to watch YouTube."

"I understand," Debbie replied. "You'll have YouTube time at our home. But while we're at Ted's, let's come up with ideas that work for you and won't agitate Ted. I think it's worth trying the video idea this time."

"I'll try it," Duncan said. "But only if I can watch YouTube videos on your phone."

"So when we get to Ted's and he tells you to go outside to play, what will you do?" Debbie asked.

"I'll tell him I hate baseball and that I need to play video games all afternoon," Duncan offered with a grin. Debbie recognized that Duncan had been trying to understand and build sarcasm into his daily routine. She thought it was a skill he was mastering.

"How very teen of you," Debbie said with a smile. "Now can you give me the real answer?"

"I'll offer to take a video of the game and I won't complain about going outside," Duncan muttered under his breath.

"Sounds like a plan."

Clarifying diverse perspectives and contexts to our children allows them to practice fitting the social behavior to the occasion. This is an incredibly important skill for navigating ever-changing social demands. Although it's helpful when family members try to understand our children and accommodate them, it's equally important for our children to learn that the thoughts, feelings, and actions of other people can be different from their own.

## Parents as advocates for their children

As parents, we are the advocates for our children in our extended families. Parents, in-laws, brothers, sisters, aunts, uncles, cousins, and grandparents can look at our kids' behavior and label it as intentional and disrespectful. Although the behavior isn't acceptable, part of my job in my extended family is to help them understand and interpret my sons' behavior so that they respond in helpful ways. I can help interpret my sons' needs and responses so that my family has the opportunity to have positive and loving relationships with my children.

### *Setting parameters for successful interactions*

What makes it so hard for us to be the expert and advocate on behalf of our children when we get back into our extended families? It can be hard to tell a parent or older sibling that they need to follow your lead when it comes to responding to your children. If your family members speak with authority, you can begin to question your ability to know anything about your child. Once we find the approaches that seem to help our children learn and function more successfully and independently, we will be bothered less by unsolicited advice. How can we remain calm when faced with potentially demanding family interactions?

STAYING CALM DURING STRESSFUL INTERACTIONS
WITH FAMILY AND FRIENDS

- *Plan a response for unsolicited advice*: Thank them for their information or concern and change the subject. Unsolicited advice can make us feel defensive and put us in debate mode over the merits of our approach. On the other hand, if you are open to suggestions and the advice seems helpful, take it!

- *Offer strategies*: Ask to have a few minutes to talk with your family when your kids aren't around to share some strategies that are working well.

- *Provide visual examples*: If your child needs a visual schedule to help her manage a new setting, bring one with you.

- *Share your "Plan B"*: It's helpful to have a back-up plan. For example, at a family reunion where people will be "hanging out" as a large group, your child could bring a book or puzzle so that he can be with everyone but doesn't have to deal with the social communication chaos.

### Parents clarify what their children need

Let's revisit our parent topic night on extended family. Suzanne, mom of 8-year-old Aaron, told the story of visiting her parents in Washington, DC. They had been at the zoo for two hours and Aaron was ready to leave.

"When are we leaving?" Aaron asked as they came up to each new exhibit. He must have asked about ten times and they hadn't responded because they were busy answering the questions his sisters had regarding the animals.

"When are we leaving?" he asked again and this time Suzanne's mom responded.

"We'll leave when we leave," she replied in an uncharacteristically exasperated tone.

"Mom," Suzanne responded, rolling her eyes and suddenly turning back into the teenage girl she had once been, "so not helpful."

"Fine," Suzanne's mom quickly responded as she walked back toward her granddaughters.

Suzanne continued, "I grabbed Aaron's hand and walked quickly toward the exit and let my mom go at a slower pace with my girls. Even though my mom's response wasn't terrible, I felt totally discouraged."

Suzanne was hoping her mom would sense what Aaron needed. But Suzanne's mom doesn't live with Aaron and so she didn't realize what approaches might work best with him. Suzanne's mom is well-intentioned but ineffective in this situation. What might have helped them all manage a demanding situation without feeling judged or patronized?

Instead of Suzanne reverting to her inner teen, she could have modeled the approach that would work with her son.

"Aaron, look at the map and tell me how many more exhibits there are in between where we are and the exit," Suzanne suggested. "Then we can guess how long that will take."

Aaron could do the math and figure out that lunch would be in approximately 15 minutes, which he could tolerate. Once Aaron was settled, Suzanne would be able to repair the relationship with her mom.

"Mom, I know your response makes sense given how many times he asked the same question," Suzanne said. "But when he asks a question that many times it's because he's trying to predict what's coming next and needs an explicit answer to help him do that. What you said didn't give him the information he needed. I'm sorry that I lost my patience with you. It's just that I only have a limited amount and I use it all up with the kids. I really need you to help keep things calm when we're all together."

As parents, we don't have all the answers and we don't always use the right approach, especially when we feel stressed or overwhelmed ourselves. However, we are aware of which strategies and language are likely to lead to learning and cooperation and which will lead to increased anxiety and meltdowns. This doesn't mean our kids always get their way— that would be a mistake. But it does mean that getting them to think flexibly and be adaptable takes more work upfront. If we share the approaches that tend to be helpful with our relatives and friends, we are increasing the chance that interactions will go more smoothly.

## Parents need to set realistic expectations for grandparents and other family members

It's very easy to blame our family members when they don't live up to our expectations about the helping role we want them to play. All of us have patterns of behavior and habits that are hard to break. If we want to have more positive interactions with our extended family, we need to either think differently about the situation or act differently in the moment. Wanting others to be different or treat us better won't make it so.

## How can we set a more positive tone in our interactions with family members?

- *Ask for what you need*: If you would like your family to listen to you without giving advice, say that at the beginning of your conversation. It's easier to hear this request before advice is offered. If you need specific help, ask for it instead of hoping your sister will read your mind and know what to offer.

- *Focus on the positive qualities*: Just as you hope that your family members will see the best in your child and appreciate the challenges he works to overcome, remember that each member in your family has their own mix of strengths and challenges too. Try to see the good in other family members instead of concentrating exclusively on their frustrating behaviors.

- *Recognize differing perspectives*: Parenting advice and norms change through the generations. What parents of young children consider crucial might not be what grandparents believe is necessary. Before judging your parents' interaction style with your children, remember that style isn't set in stone, nor is there only one way to interact with children.

### Favoritism rears its ugly head

Let's return to another topic night for grandparents and hear some of their concerns. Marilyn, whose 11-year-old grandson, Brian, has Asperger's, came to her first event at AANE with lots of Kleenex, frustration, sadness, and anger.

"I feel terrible saying this, but I can't relate to my grandson," Marilyn said. "He's into all these games I don't understand and that's all he wants to do. I can't take him out to the movies because he just covers his ears and screams. I can't take him out to eat because he'll run out of the restaurant. He doesn't like the beach and asks when we're going home when we've only been there for ten minutes. I don't know what to do with him."

## Like attracts like

Marilyn is experiencing what many parents and grandparents experience when they have a child or grandchild with divergent interests from the family norm. In her case, all her grandson likes is Pokémon and the game doesn't make sense to her. She doesn't want to join him in his game world, but would rather that he could join her in her family's sense of fun. How frustrating it must be to want to share an activity with your grandchild, only to find out that your idea of fun and his couldn't be more different. Let's rejoin Marilyn as she continues.

"I love spending time with Brian's younger sister, Katie," Marilyn continued. "She smiles at me and asks me lots of questions and likes to hear stories. I almost feel like I have to tell my son that I can take Katie and not Brian on the weekend. I don't want them to think I don't love Brian—of course I do. I just don't know how to relate to him and I don't want him to limit what Katie and I can do together. I also think that Katie is put second so often in the family because Brian needs so much. Since Brian doesn't like movies, Katie doesn't get to go to movies. Our beach days are shortened because of Brian, even though Katie enjoys playing in the sand and the waves. I want to give Katie some of the experiences her parents can't because it's too stressful for Brian. Is that wrong?"

It makes sense that Marilyn is going to relate more easily to the grandchild who shares her interests. It is also nice that she wants to give Katie some one-on-one time. Marilyn might want to talk with her son about taking each child separately so that they each get alone time with grandma without Marilyn having to negotiate such divergent interests and needs in one visit.

How to relate to your grandchild when your
interests are completely different

- *Start where your grandchild is*: If your grandchild has an interest that isn't familiar to you, start learning about it. Ask your grandchild questions about the interest. Try to listen when they talk about it. Offer to watch them play a game or ask them to teach you how to play.

- *Learn about Asperger's (or related diagnosis)*: You won't take behavioral challenges personally when you understand why your grandchild struggles with certain social expectations.

- *Focus on your grandchild's strengths*: It's easy to compare a grandchild with challenges to a typically developing grandchild and expect them to behave as their typical siblings or cousins. Focus on what they are capable of and interactions that include their interests and they enjoy.

- *Make family outings work for all*: Make sure to have activities or supplies to help your grandchild with Asperger's manage the demands of the day. That might mean making a schedule ahead of time, bringing special foods, having games she likes, making music or videos available, allowing breaks from large crowds, and having a "Plan B" for when a complete change of venue is needed.

### Sharing joy and celebrating relatives' accomplishments

Let's rejoin the topic night on extended family and hear Martha's reaction to her niece's accomplishments.

"My sister's children are skilled athletes and are probably going to college on athletic scholarships," Martha explained. "My daughter trips walking through the halls of her high school. My sister's daughters have large groups of friends from their softball and swim teams. They don't ever seem to be at a loss for companionship. My daughter locks herself in her bedroom and doesn't get a phone call or text. I want to be a good aunt and sister. I want to be happy for them and celebrate their success. But inside, I feel like someone punched me in the gut every time another athletic accomplishment is brought up in conversation. I know, in my heart, my sister doesn't mean any of this to hurt, but I can't help feeling more isolated and disconnected from her and my nieces after we are together. How can I be happy for them without feeling like my own daughter is being left behind?"

Martha is bringing up a very common feeling for parents. Hearing of other's accomplishments in areas where our own children are less adept is difficult. It doesn't mean we don't want our relatives to have successes, but it can be painful each time we are reminded that our children are growing and developing on different trajectories, and the timelines that apply to typically developing children won't make sense for our kids. Some of this discomfort can arise from a discrepancy in what will be seen as an accomplishment for our children versus what will be shared from other family members. When typically developing children learn to ride a bike, have a sleepover, have friends to hang out with, tie their shoes, learn to drive, or move away for college or work, we see that as their expected path. It's something to celebrate, but not a huge surprise, and didn't require more than the usual amount of energy and effort to accomplish the task. When our children with Asperger's accomplish these goals, it's a huge accomplishment, worthy of "jumping for joy" because the amount of effort required far exceeded what is typically called for and we didn't know if these milestones would be met. So how can we help ourselves manage the emotions that overtake us as we are continually faced with reminders that our children won't be on the same path as some of their relatives?

MANAGING OUR EMOTIONS AS WE CELEBRATE OTHERS'
DEVELOPMENTAL MILESTONES AND ACCOMPLISHMENTS

- *Throw away the yardstick*: Our children are on their own trajectory for their social and emotional development. They may not meet the same timelines as typically developing children, but their growth and development continues into adulthood (Drezner 2012).

- *Alter your perspective*: Remember that many children struggle with some aspect of growth and development. Just because you don't see what's hard for someone else's child, it doesn't mean it doesn't exist. Parenting isn't easy for anyone.

- *Distraction can be positive*: It can be restorative to take a break from our own concerns and focus on the joys of another family member.

## Parents build their friendship networks

As parents we often find friends through the schools our children attend and their activities. It's wonderful when these types of friendships are enjoyable, healthy, and supportive. At times, our friendship network might be lacking depth and be composed of acquaintances who make us feel depleted. So how do we develop friendships that are healthy and minimize those who are potentially poisonous to our well-being?

### Toxic friendships for parents

When my oldest son was 3, he was already reading. One of my friends came over and saw Noah reading a book out loud on the sofa.

"How did you teach him to read?" Miranda wanted to know.

"I didn't," I responded. "He just picked it up." "You must have done something," Miranda continued. "How much did you read to him each day? How did you read to him? Do you ask him questions as you read? Did you point to words? Holly's as smart as Noah. I want her to be able to read if he's reading. How can I teach her to read as a 3-year-old?" Miranda asked in rapid-fire succession.

"I gave him the gift of Asperger's," I responded in an exasperated tone. "Sometimes it includes reading early. The thing is, you don't get to choose which parts of Asperger's you get. So if Holly gets the gift of early reading, she might also get difficulty with reading social cues or managing her emotions."

Miranda looked at me blankly. She didn't get that she'd crossed a line and I wasn't sure she was a friend that I needed to try and keep.

"I don't know how to teach children how to read early," I continued. "My guess is Holly will learn to read on her own timetable and comparing her to Noah isn't a good idea."

"Well I'm going to do some research into teaching children to read early. If Noah can do it, I'm sure Holly can too," Miranda responded, not able to set aside her wishes for her daughter's success in being a star reader.

Although these were early clues that Miranda and I were not destined to be life-long friends, I kept thinking our relationship would become more reciprocal over time and that her sensitivity she'd shown toward strangers in need would transfer to me. I was wrong. Miranda was visiting one day with her baby when the early interventionist was working with Noah. Miranda gladly showed off her new daughter, Shauna, to our home visitor. The home visitor responded with, "It's so nice to see a normal baby smiling and cooing. I don't get to experience that very much because all the children I work with have disabilities and they don't do all the normal things you expect on time like smiling and crawling. I could play with her all day."

"You can play with her all you want," offered Miranda beaming at the praise as Noah and I sat in the background waiting for his session to continue. Neither Miranda nor the home visitor had noticed we were in earshot or thought that this conversation might make us feel like second-class citizens who might never attain the preferred status of normal.

It was at that moment, when Miranda didn't respond with care or check in with me after the home visitor left, that I knew I wouldn't be continuing to see her. I wasn't in the right frame of mind to handle her unintended insensitivity. When deciding on which friends to keep in your inner circle, it can be helpful to keep the following in mind.

### Key points for healthy friendships for parents

- *Shared understanding*: Look for parents who seem to understand what it's like for you and your family. Often this means finding other parents who are also raising a child with Asperger's. It can also mean parents who are good listeners, don't judge, and aren't trying to compare their child with yours.

- *Reciprocity exists*: Friendships flourish when there is give and take from both sides. This doesn't mean the help, support, or interaction has to be of the same type, but if you start to feel resentment over long-term lopsidedness, you may want to consider giving the relationship a rest or talking to your friend about your concerns.

- *Shared interests*: When you have something in common with potential friends, you're more likely to enjoy time together. You can search out connections by joining groups, organizations, and houses of worship, or volunteering for programs that share your values.

- *Know when to say goodbye*: If a friend is causing you great stress and you don't think you can repair the relationship, it might be time to shift your efforts to other relationships.

## Setting panic aside

We carry a suitcase full of expectations for our families, our friends, and ourselves. Communicating our needs and concerns clearly helps our family and friends understand our perspective. Remember that all of us are doing the best we can with the skills and abilities we have at any point in time.

CHAPTER 7 ——————————————————

# Siblings

Parents rarely feel as if they have enough time for all their children. There's always a sense of a child with Asperger's needing more and a hope that the other children in the family will manage well enough with what's left.

Realistic expectations are a good first step. Expecting perfection is a recipe for disaster for any family, but especially one with Asperger's thrown into the mix. Our families need flexibility, understanding, patience, and humor. No single person in the family is to blame for difficulties—how we work together and relate to each other will make situations better or worse. Helping siblings understand how we can all collaborate as a family gives everyone the right amount of power and control.

So, where do we start when questions and concerns about siblings bubble up? We begin with normalizing Asperger's. This means Asperger's is part of our family constellation—something we need to learn about and understand. Without that understanding siblings will struggle with our actions, which might be perceived as unfair or preferential.

Throughout this chapter on siblings, you will learn that:

- understanding Asperger's helps you to:
  - build compassion and flexibility among siblings
  - anticipate and plan for challenging situations

- decide which activities are right for your child and family

• balancing expectations for you and your children helps you to:
  - address issues of fairness
  - teach daily survival skills, like waiting without whining and banishing boredom
  - allow children to pursue other interests and express concerns

• sibling mistreatment can decrease by helping your children:
  - learn how to manage overwhelming emotions
  - develop the ability to see another person's point of view
  - understand the unwritten rules of the family
  - respect each other's need for privacy.

First, let's start with exploring how understanding Asperger's is the essential building block for increasing family harmony.

## Normalizing Asperger's in our families

One of the most-asked questions at topic nights is how to help brothers and sisters understand their sibling with Asperger's. Lisa, a parent of three children, started the discussion.

"My other kids, who are 8 and 10, complain all the time about 7-year-old Jeremy," Lisa said. "Jeremy throws tantrums when we're out in public. Last week we were at a football game and the noise was bothering Jeremy—he started screaming and wouldn't stop. I couldn't leave the other kids in the stands while I left, so we all had to leave. That's when my 10-year-old piped up."

"I'm not going!" John screamed. "I want to watch the game. We always have to leave early because of Jeremy. He's a baby. I hate him."

"John, I'm sorry—we have to go," Lisa replied softly. She saw that her 8-year-old daughter, Samantha, was looking at the ground, probably hoping to disappear into it.

"No way—Jeremy always gets his way," John said. "I'm not going. You can take him out. But I'm staying until the end."

## Understanding Asperger's builds compassion and flexibility

Like many parents, Lisa hadn't talked to her children about Asperger's yet, so they didn't realize that Jeremy has significant sensory regulation issues that make loud and crowded events a challenging experience for him. If the whole family knew why these events were so difficult and painful for Jeremy, they might make different choices about who attends or how long they stay. Because none of this is clear in this moment, John is left feeling disappointed and angry. He believes that his mom bends to Jeremy's tantrums and maybe he should have a tantrum of his own to get his way just this once. Now, let's return to Lisa and John and see how she handles John's anger and confusion.

"John, I need you to do this," Lisa explained. "I am sorry. You have every right to be upset with Jeremy and me. But I need your help. Just come out with me now and maybe you'll be able to come back in after Jeremy calms down."

"No," John answered. "Jeremy always gets what he wants. You always take his side. When do I get what I want? What makes him so special?"

Lisa felt as if she was going to explode. Jeremy was still screaming. People in the stands were looking at her to do something. John wasn't moving. Samantha quietly stood up and started toward the exit.

"John, get up," Lisa seethed under her breath. "We're leaving now. No more discussion. We can talk about it in the car."

We've all been in these types of situations—stuck in a public place with children who won't do what we ask. John's feelings have overwhelmed him and he's trying to take a stand. Lisa feels like a failure and just needs everyone to cooperate. How can we help our children understand why situations like these are challenging and what we can all do to lower the stress?

### Explaining Asperger's to your other children

- *Disclosure to siblings*: Once your child understands his own diagnosis, you can explain Asperger's to your other children. Providing information helps your children understand their sibling's behavior and keeps them from creating their own (often incorrect and negative) explanations for it.

- *Use books/videos*: Just as parents feel better when they know they aren't alone in the parenting challenges they face, our children benefit from knowing there are other children who understand what it's like to live with a brother or sister on the autism spectrum. Coulter Videos created a DVD, *Understanding Brothers and Sisters With Asperger Syndrome* (Coulter 2007). Sam Frender and his mother, Robin Schiffmiller, wrote the book, *Brotherly Feelings: Me, My Emotions, and My Brother with Asperger Syndrome* (Frender and Schiffmiller 2007).

- *Professional help*: Sometimes parents involve a family therapist who understands Asperger's to help with disclosing to siblings. Some join sibling groups to be around other brothers and sisters who understand what their life is like.

## Understanding Asperger's allows you to anticipate and plan for challenging situations

Once you and your family understand Asperger's better, you'll be able to be more proactive in your planning of family events and outings.

PRACTICAL STRATEGIES FOR MANAGING
DIVERSE NEEDS AND INTERESTS

- *Separate siblings occasionally*: My younger children wanted to go to Legoland in Florida and Noah wasn't interested. I let Noah stay home with his dad and I took Daniel and Josh. It was a wonderful trip because it suited Daniel and Josh, and we weren't trying to make Noah fit into a situation that would've made him uncomfortable. It's not always possible to separate siblings for events and outings, but if you can find another adult to help out (co-parent, spouse, friend, another relative, or a sitter), you can enjoy the event with your children who are excited to attend.

- *Seek out accommodations*: If your child is interested in attending an event, but doesn't like loud noises or crowds, consider bringing noise cancelling headphones or earplugs. Call the venue to inquire about accommodations.

- *Find a co-leader*: Join with another family so that you have another adult to share the responsibility of watching children. If you need to leave with your child, another trusted adult could stay with the other children.

- *Utilize distractions*: Have your child bring along activities he likes so that he can be distracted by a book, video game, or other enticement while the rest of the family pays attention to the actual event. I usually have my kids bring books when we attend something that might not appeal to them.

- *Take turns*: If you are going to an event that has a variety of activities available, make a list of choices and have your children help prioritize which they want to attend. Show them that everyone will get their first choice and that they will have to wait when it's not their turn. Giving choices and making a list takes the element of surprise out of the event and helps all children understand how the time will flow.

*Understanding Asperger's helps you decide which activities are right for your child with AS and her siblings*

It can be very challenging to find activities that work well for all your children. I certainly felt as if there were years in which anytime we tried to do anything out of the ordinary with all three of my children, it was a huge mistake. It can take tremendous energy to corral a group of kids with divergent abilities and interests into a cohesive unit and have them enjoy time together.

HOW DO YOU DECIDE WHICH ACTIVITIES ARE RIGHT
FOR YOUR CHILD WITH AS AND HER SIBLINGS?

- *Find commonality*: Start where your children are—is there anything they already like to do together? My three boys will watch movies or play board games together. A few years ago, they were all curled up on the sofa together under a blanket laughing at a movie together and I ran and got Jed to show him, because it was such a rare occurrence. Once you recognize any common ground for siblings, offer continued opportunities for them to interact in a positive way with each other.

- *Recognize what works at home*: If you have more than two children, you can help all your children recognize what activities they can do with each of their siblings. Maybe your child with AS likes to play cards with one sibling and likes to listen to music with another. They don't all have to enjoy the same activities with every member of the family. You may even want to make a list to help each of your children see what activities are likely to work with different siblings.

- *Recognize what works away from home*: It also helps to brainstorm a list of activities or outings that are likely to be successful with all your children and which might work better with fewer of them. For our kids, we've learned that we can all hike together. If we choose to bike instead, it needs to be much shorter to be successful for all. Any activity requiring extensive time in the water won't work for Noah, but Daniel and Josh are part fish. We've learned to compromise and clarify up front how long an activity will take and be open to suggestions from our kids on how to make it work for everyone.

- *Therapeutic support*: If your child with AS is working with a therapist to help with emotional regulation or thinking flexibly, the therapist could assign "homework" to have your child practice coping strategies when frustrated by siblings or activities. Your child can rate the effectiveness of the strategies in the real world and create a list of effective approaches.

Next, let's join other parents at a recent topic night to see how the roles and expectations we place on our children and ourselves may lead to imbalance and learn how we can correct it to stay upright.

## Balancing responsibilities in the family

David, a father attending his first topic night, raised his concern.

"My son with Asperger's is 9 years old. His brother is 7. I see my 7-year-old trying to take care of my 9-year-old. It's like he's becoming a third parent in the house. I want to encourage my boys to get along, but when will the older one be able to help the younger one?"

Marcia, a mom with four kids, chimed in with her experience. "Justine, my 14-year-old, was screaming at me yesterday because I asked her to come home right after school and watch her 12-year-old brother with Asperger's." She proceeded to replay their conversation.

"No way, Mom," Justine screamed. "I stayed home by myself when I was 12. He can stay home by himself too. Just let him play video games."

"Justine, I need you to do this," Marcia explained. "Tyler's never stayed home by himself for more than a few minutes. You've never complained before. What's happening now?"

"I was going over to a friend's house after school," Justine cried. "I shouldn't have to give up going to a friend's house because of Tyler. I'm sick of taking care of him."

"Justine, I'm sorry, but I need you to do this," Marcia said softly. "We'll figure out something else soon, but tomorrow, please just do what I asked."

Marcia paused, before continuing, "I have no idea if I handled that okay or not. I mean, Tyler's 12 and he does need someone with him. But Justine's right, I depend on her all the time and it's too much for her."

It's not strange that we would want some assistance from our neurotypical kids in the day-to-day demands of our households. It also makes sense that we would like our children with Asperger's to be involved in household responsibilities. How do we find balance to ensure that our children have responsibilities that help the family function but don't take on parental roles prematurely?

### Balancing responsibilities requires discussion, negotiation, and planning

How we talk with our children about our expectations and needs matters. Our words have the potential to make our children feel appreciated and understood *or* taken for granted. Siblings have the longest relationship of any family member. We don't want our children growing up thinking that they have to sacrifice all their own interests for the sake of their sibling with Asperger's. At the same time, some of the most compassionate and vocal advocates in the autism spectrum community are siblings. So how do we foster compassion and minimize resentment?

- *Discuss, don't demand*: When I need help from my kids, we consult the calendar to consider what types of events are already set (homework, activities, and time with friends). I might say, "I have an appointment after school on Thursday and could use your help watching your brothers. Would that work for you?" This type of language doesn't demand or assume participation. Usually if I phrase my request as, "This would mean a lot to me," or "You'd be helping me out and I really appreciate it," my child is more likely to help without feeling annoyed.

- *Watching siblings is a job*: Check your older child's availability and pay her for her time. I made the rule that I would pay when the time exceeded an hour. My older kids like making money and would take the job seriously. Resentment decreased when I offered the incentive of money and we negotiated dates and times.

- *Plan for fun*: Make sure all the children in the family get to pursue their interests. It's easy to focus all your energy on the child with special needs. Focus on the other children too. Give them your attention and time to see what they like. In my family of three kids, each child gets to pick one activity they want to do. They are often involved in more than one activity, but they each get a say about one thing they are interested in and would enjoy.

- *Make jobs visual and rotate if possible*: Have family meetings to discuss family responsibilities. Each child's jobs or responsibilities might look different depending on age and ability. One child might feed the family pet. One might set the table. One might clean up after dinner. Let the whole family see that we are in this together and we all help; that's just part of being in our family. This keeps resentment from building as the siblings see that everyone has a job to fit their capabilities—no one is left off. We sometimes had a job chart or calendar, like the one in Table 7.1, so that the division of job responsibilities was clear. This helped whenever one child would grouse, "Why doesn't Daniel have to clear the table?" I could easily respond, "Oh, I guess you forgot that we all have jobs. This week, you're clearing the table and Daniel's feeding the dog. Next week you switch."

**Table 7.1**: Household jobs

| Job | Who is responsible for the job this week? |
| --- | --- |
| Setting the table for dinner | Noah |
| Feeding the dog breakfast | Josh |
| Feeding the dog dinner | Daniel |

- *Recognize successes*: Celebrate times when your children work well together. Our kids are happy to take care of our dog most of the time. I compliment them on how their actions help our dog stay healthy and happy. I also point out that because they have taken on the main responsibility of caring for our dog, I can do other things for our family, like cook dinner. Pointing out how assisting each other makes the family run more smoothly makes kids more aware of the helping role they play in the family.

- *Encourage sibling support, not surrogate parenting*: It's easy to slide toward asking our children to take on ever-increasing responsibilities for their sibling with AS. Although we want to encourage our children to be supportive and helpful with each other, we don't want to deputize one of them to be the caretaker. Encouraging support to flow in both directions helps all our children feel that they are seen as individuals and their needs are taken into account.

If we want to find the right balance for our kids in helping their siblings, let's bring them into the discussion. We can't turn them into another parent—that's our job. And if we need more help than our children can provide, we need to seek other avenues to build a supportive structure.

### Balancing the needs of all our children is challenging

Many parents wish they were able to give the same amount of time and attention to all their kids. So often we are trying to balance everyone's needs and activities and it can feel as if we are never doing enough, or the right thing, for any of our children, whether they have Asperger's or not. The last thing we want to do is make any of our kids think that the only way they get our attention is by having a crisis.

A few years ago I went to a conference and listened to a professional and parent of three children talk about how she handled this constant feeling of not being a "good enough" parent. She said that, although one of her three children had Asperger's, she worked very hard to make sure that her other children got time and attention too. This meant that sometimes her son with Asperger's had to wait for her or her husband's attention. They worked hard to teach him that he wasn't the only one in the family with needs, and that the parents did need to let the other kids talk at the dinner table, have friends over, and attend parent–teacher conferences and concerts. I remember tears welling up as she spoke because I was struggling with this and felt as if I was a complete failure as a parent. I felt that my oldest son required my constant assistance, and yet I had two other children who had needs too. How could I possibly be fair, loving, and attentive to all of them? I started to resent the typical needs of all children, because I felt as if they kept me from "working with" my oldest child. These are terrible and intense feelings that can suck all the joy out of having a family. Attending that lecture was an "aha" moment for me. I started to think about how I might be able to help my oldest son learn to wait and engage more with his siblings, instead of me always feeling that there wasn't enough of me to go around.

## How to balance the needs of multiple children

- *Waiting without whining*: Teach your child with Asperger's about waiting. Waiting is a hard concept to master—we all struggle with it at times. Waiting is particularly hard for a child with Asperger's because it is unstructured and open-ended. How long will you have to wait? What are you supposed to do as you wait? What happens if you start something and your "waiting time" is done and you have to stop what you're doing quickly? We have to be explicit about what people do while they wait so that we help our kids learn how to manage this open-ended timeframe. When my kids were younger, they used a "While I Wait Book," to help them know what their choices were. It included pictures of options they might choose, like looking at trading cards, playing with toy cars, doing a dot-to-dot, or talking to me. Now that they are older, they usually read or listen to music.

- *One-on-one*: Find some way to have one-on-one time with each child. I know it is hard to do, but it is one of the best ways to connect to each individual child. Depending on what your kids like, you can go for a walk, play a game, cook together, swim, sing, draw, or watch a movie together. What you do is not that important; it's the time together without siblings taking over that matters. I try to do this each week with each child for a short amount of time. I might take advantage of the time one child is doing an activity and take the other one out for a snack or to the library while we wait. Sometimes our time together is just walking the dog around the block so that I can listen without interruption. Think of moments during the day where you can tune into each child. If you get a longer outing together, that's great, but not necessary to help all your kids feel connected to you.

- *Talk time*: Give all the kids equal talk time. In our house, our oldest son can monopolize the conversation easily at any meal or time we're all together. We point out to him that there are five people at the table and so all five people need to get an equal share of the "talk time." For a while we used a ball at the table as the "talk ball." When you had the talk ball that meant you could share what you wanted to talk about.

- *Game night*: We just started "family game night" once a week. Each week a different child picks the game. This keeps us from playing the same game repeatedly and everyone gets a chance to choose. We play the game for a short amount of time so that we can end on a good note.

- *Encourage children not to hide their needs*: Sometimes siblings will hide or minimize their own problems because they don't think their parents can handle additional concerns (Rubin 2013). We have to send the clear message that we don't expect or need any of our children to be perfect. At times we might not feel up to the challenge of multiple children with multiple needs, but our children need us to accept them as they are.

So far, we've discussed understanding Asperger's and providing balance in the family. For the last topic, we're going to consider why siblings mistreat each other and how we can support a more thoughtful and responsive approach to disagreement and anger that arises between siblings. Let's join William as he laments how his children talk to each other.

## Sibling mistreatment

At another sibling topic night, William was worried about how his sons talked to each other.

"My 10-year-old is so mean to his younger brother. All he does is yell at him and call him a moron. No matter how many times I tell Jason not to be mean, he just keeps doing it. Last night at bedtime, my 7-year-old asked why Jason hates him so much. I didn't have an answer."

### Sibling mistreatment cause 1: emotional regulation and perspective-taking challenges

It is normal for siblings to hold dichotomous feelings about each other. They can love and hate simultaneously. They may want to be with their siblings *and* wish they would go away. The feelings are acceptable; it's the behavior that can be the problem. What can make this challenging in a child with AS, is that often our kids don't have well-developed emotional regulation skills. They aren't yet able to modulate the strong emotions they feel. It's hard to be reasonable in your response to a bothersome sibling if you don't have evenhanded responses for more mundane irritations.

Perspective taking also affects your child's ability to recognize that a younger or older sibling will have different interests and abilities. Here's a typical exchange between two of my three kids.

"I like *Phineas and Ferb*," offers 6-year-old Josh.

"*Phineas and Ferb* is stupid," replies 14-year-old Noah.

"It is not."

"Yes, it is. You're an idiot."

"No. You're an idiot."

You get the sense of the valuable discourse that occurs each night at dinner! We try to talk about other things, but we often end up with this.

"What's 10 plus 10?" asks Josh.

"That's so easy," Noah responds glibly. "Why don't you ask a real question?"

"Just answer!" screams Josh.

"No, it's a dumb question." Noah replies as he holds firm in his resolve not to enjoy interacting with his brother.

### Sibling mistreatment solution 1: facilitating emotional regulation and perspective taking

It seems like a typical fight between siblings, but there's an extra piece. I need to check that my son with Asperger's understands what we call "ages and stages."

"Are 6-year-olds the same as 14-year-olds?" I ask.

Noah smiles at me. He notices I haven't chastised him for being mean to his brother yet. I rephrase the question.

"Do 6-year-olds look the same as 14-year-olds?"

Noah's smile widens. "No," he replies with the tone of "duh."

I have my oldest and youngest son stand next to each other and take a picture. *Thank you camera phone.* I show them the picture.

"Could you two be mistaken for twins?" I ask as they look at the picture.

"No way!" They both laugh.

"Do 6-year-olds and 14-year-olds learn the same things in school?"

"No."

"Should we expect 6-year-olds to know all the things that 14-year-olds know?"

"No."

"So when a 6-year-old is excited about what he's learning and wants to share it with his family, how should we respond?"

"Fine. I get it," scowls Noah as the message starts to get through.

"You know you can think whatever you want about your brothers," I say. "I'm not in charge of your thoughts. But if you don't edit what you think before you talk, what will your brothers think about you?"

"They'll think I hate them," he replies under his breath.

"Do you realize how devastating that can be for your brothers?" I ask. "They want to be with you. But when you talk to them that way they believe you hate them. Is that what you want them to think about you?"

"No."

"I know you care about your brothers," I explain. "Whenever they are hurt, you are nice to them and ask if they are okay. But when you're frustrated with them, your response is unnecessarily harsh. Let's see if we can come up with other things you can say in the moment when your brothers frustrate you."

"I don't want to do that now," Noah complains.

"Well, we need to come up with some ideas today," I explain. "You pick the time. I think it will take five minutes."

"After dinner," Noah offers.

"That's fine."

Even though I may want to have the conversation about the need for my kids to change their behavior as the problem behavior happens, they usually can't do it right then. They're too worked up and upset, and can't really think creatively to solve the problem in the moment. Making appointments to talk about the issue later works better. I don't ask when they "want" to talk about it, as they can easily get stuck on the word "want," and then their response is very predictable, "I don't want to talk about it." Having them pick a time later in the day for a short five-minute conversation is likely to work better.

### Sibling mistreatment cause 2: unwritten rules of siblinghood

When my oldest son was in fifth grade, he became quite adept at fighting with his brothers. One day I asked him, "Why do you fight so much?"

"That's what brothers are supposed to do," he replied a bit too quickly.

"Seriously, why do you fight with your brothers?" I tried again.

"Because," Noah said more slowly and with greater emphasis, "we're brothers—that's what we do." His face showed no sense of irony or sarcasm, which he had been learning about and trying to use with increased frequency.

"Fair enough," I said. "Brothers fight. But what about all the other things that brothers are supposed to do together?"

"There isn't anything else we're supposed to do together," Noah declared. "We're brothers. We fight. That's what we do."

The conversation was clearly over for the time being. I wasn't going to get more out of him in that moment. But what became clear from that brief interaction was that he was missing valuable information about sibling relationships. Yes, he was absolutely correct, brothers do fight. But that's not all they do and he wasn't aware of what he didn't know. He hadn't remembered all the times he and his brothers had gotten along without complaint. He was missing the "hidden curriculum," the implicit, unwritten social rules that govern behavior (Myles *et al.* 2004). Now it was time to teach him possibilities he hadn't imagined or remembered from previous experiences.

### Sibling mistreatment solution 2: explaining the unwritten rules of siblinghood

It's usually helpful to use visual aids in addition to talking to your children. So I created a pie chart (Figure 7.1). All the boys thought it was hilarious, but it made the point very clear. Brothers do a variety of things together, not just fight. Brothers can play together, help each other, and, one of my personal favorites as a sibling, join together to plot against the parents. Once my boys saw the chart, we started talking about the different things they already do that fit into different categories. They were able to come up with activities they all enjoy—playing video games, watching movies, going on hikes, walking to get ice-cream, playing board games, playing with the dog, making comics, or co-existing in the same space peacefully for more than a few minutes. The visual display helped them to see how much time "should" be devoted to the different types of activities. Fighting is a smaller slice of the pie because we agree that it's a part of having siblings, but it's not the largest part. Playing and helping each other are larger slices of the pie because we want to encourage those types of interactions. The pie chart didn't resolve all the strong feelings my kids have about each other, but it was a way for them to understand the hidden curriculum of having siblings and what we as a family are working toward.

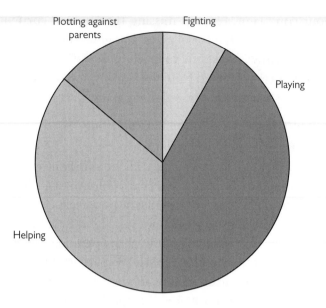

**Figure 7.1**: What siblings do together

### Sibling mistreatment cause 3: privacy needs

Tony Attwood, in his book, *The Complete Guide to Asperger's Syndrome*, explains the importance of privacy for people with Asperger's: "Solitude is one of the most effective emotional restoratives for someone with Asperger's syndrome. Being alone can be a very effective way of calming down and is also enjoyable, especially if engaged in a special interest" (Attwood 2007, pp.55–56).

Often, parents ask how to handle one sibling who wants privacy and another who can't imagine being alone. We experience that in our house too. The oldest child wants time alone, and the youngest wants to be wherever the oldest one is. It is okay for children to want privacy. If they aren't ever allowed to have time alone, they will react negatively toward their brother or sister every time they try to play or get the older sibling's attention. Children will not, nor should they be required to, be together always. Time away from siblings won't always be an option, but we can try to build it into our schedules so that our kids see that we take the need for alone time seriously.

*Sibling mistreatment solution 3a: structuring time for privacy*
One of the easiest solutions is to have doorknob hangers or signs on each bedroom. One side says, "Do not enter," or "Privacy please," depending on how polite you feel like being. The other side says, "Please come in," or "Safe to enter." After each child makes a sign, talk about when and how to use it. In our house, when your doorknob hanger shows, "Do not enter," that means the person in the room needs privacy. To make sure my kids understand what we've just talked about, I have them explain it back to me.

"Tell me how we use the doorknob hangers," I say to all the kids.

"Everybody puts them on their door and then you decide which side to show," they respond.

"If the do-not-enter side is showing, what does that mean?"

"It means you can't go in that room," they answer.

"What else does it mean?" I ask. "It means you can't just sit outside the door and call their name over and over," Josh answers.

"What about knocking on the door?"

"You can knock on the door, but you can't go in unless the person says it's okay," Daniel clarifies.

"So what will you do instead?"

"I have to pick something else to do," Josh answers.

"What are some other good choices?"

"I don't know," Daniel admits.

"Hmmm, how about reading books?" I offer.

"Okay," all boys nod in agreement.

"Or you like Lego and puzzles. Those are things you can do by yourself if no one else can play with you."

"I can try," Josh says ready to be done with the conversation.

### Sibling mistreatment solution 3b: privacy needs and structuring unstructured time

Making the signs is the first step in guaranteeing some privacy. But our kids have a hard time knowing how to handle "down time" if they can't do the thing they most want to do (annoy or be with their sibling). We have to help them see that they have options. We can create a book with pictures that reminds them of what they like to do. We could have a list in their room that helps them remember what types of activities they can do when they don't have a sibling or parent with whom to interact. Giving them the list they helped create can help them remember that they do like to read by themselves, make paper airplanes, build with Lego, or listen to music.

We can also explain to our children that time alone and privacy are important. We can't always have it the minute we need it, but it can be built into the day. When our kids were younger, we used to have "quiet or alone time," which meant that everyone was in their own room, or if they shared a bedroom with a sibling, they might use my bedroom, doing some quiet activity or resting. It doesn't mean hours of spa-like rejuvenation, but quiet time allowed everyone to have a break from each other. It's helpful to have time each day where siblings get a break from interacting with each other. When you're in a family with multiple children, that's important.

### Sibling mistreatment cause 4: the fairness dilemma

Fairness is a concept that comes up in every topic night on siblings. When you have multiple children and one of them has Asperger's, you will have some different rules, approaches, consequences, and supports in place because all your children *need* different things. When you have Asperger's in the family, trying to treat everyone uniformly creates immense stress and leads to failure and frustration because it doesn't work.

Children notice when a sibling gets something (or gets away with something) they don't; whether it is attention, food, an activity, a toy, or expectations for consistent behavior. My goal when addressing concerns or issues of fairness isn't to get all children to agree with me, but I hope that they will understand why each family member may have different needs and, as a result of these unique needs, may require individualized approaches and consequences. These are not one-shot conversations. Learning and accepting why some members of the family really do live by different rules takes time.

*Sibling mistreatment solution 4: explaining fairness*
Here's how I like to talk about fairness with kids.

"What does it mean when something is fair?" I ask.

"It means that everyone gets the same thing," my kids reply without skipping a beat.

"That's not the definition I know," I say. "Being fair means that everyone gets what they need. You all have different needs, so what you get will be different. Fair doesn't mean the same."

My kids do not look at all convinced with my logic. They are getting ready to argue with me about what they need; I can see it. I launch into the bike-riding description.

"Josh is learning to ride his bike and so he and I go out for ten minutes every day to practice. Should all of you go so that I can be fair?"

The kids all smile and laugh at my unrealistic request. "No way, we already know how to ride our bikes. That's stupid."

"I agree. It would be stupid. But if you think fair means that everyone gets the same, then if I'm spending time teaching Josh to ride, I should spend time teaching you all to ride too."

"But we don't need to learn to ride. We know how to ride!" the older boys scream at me.

"So, if I follow your logic, I shouldn't make you all do or get the same things to be fair. If you don't need something, I shouldn't make you do it."

Uh-oh. The boys are scrunching their faces. They don't like how the conversation has turned.

"Look, you will all get what you need. I promise to do my best for that. But you don't all need the same things and so you won't all get the same things—whether it's a type of food, a new toy, teaching you a skill, or jobs you do around the house. We can always talk about what each of you needs, and sometimes you will get the same things, but sometimes you won't, and that's okay."

"I still don't think it's fair," my middle son piped up.

"That's alright. You don't have to like it, but I think you understand it, and that's good enough for now."

Usually after a discussion like this one, I will try to do something with the boys that they enjoy. Getting these concepts into their heads is tricky and it helps to have something to look forward to, like letting them show me their favorite computer game. It also helps my head not explode, which feels like a real possibility at times!

## Key tips about siblings

- *Find activities that work with all your kids*: It might only be one or two things, but help them see that they can enjoy being with each other.

- *Time-limit full family activities for success*: If you are heading to an event or activity, have an exit strategy so that when your child with AS (or any of your children) have had enough, you can leave or provide distractions or alternatives. Don't choose activities that aren't a good fit for the current capacities of your kids if you have a choice.

- *Normalize Asperger's*: Learn how Asperger's affects your child and explain this to your other children in age-appropriate language.

- *Support privacy*: Build quiet time into your day, when possible, so that your kids can get a break from being with each other. If one child really needs "alone" time, make that a priority.

- *Teach how to ignore*: Children with Asperger's find it very difficult to ignore the annoying behavior of siblings. Instead of telling them to "ignore it," we need to offer concrete alternatives, like walking away, asking for help, going to their own room for privacy, or offering to do something that will be less annoying with their sibling.

- *Make family jobs and responsibilities explicit*: Give children a choice about which job to do, when possible. Limit the number of jobs and amount of time each job takes so that each child can be successful.

- *Spend some one-on-one time with each child*: This can be time together while you are running an errand or making dinner.

- *Learn to stay calm*: To help your child manage their large emotions, teach and practice coping and calming strategies (see Chapter 3 for specific examples).

- *Interpret siblings' behavior for your child with AS when necessary*: Often our kids with AS don't understand why their siblings act as they do and get irritable as a result. They may not agree with our interpretation, but it's a start to help them gain the perspective they currently lack.

- *Encourage your children to be themselves*: All children need to be allowed to express their concerns and share their problems. We need to send the clear message that our children are accepted as they are and that we don't need or expect them to be perfect.

## Setting panic aside

Parenting multiple kids is challenging and wonderful at the same time. Just as our kids can feel love and hate at the same time for their siblings, we can feel overwhelmed and grateful simultaneously. Remember that no individual can meet *all* the needs of each family member *all* the time. But we can create a safe space where siblings know they are loved for who they are and not what they do.

CHAPTER 8 ─────────────────────────────

# Holidays and Vacations

We've all seen the advertisements for family fun. Smiling children and parents with their arms around one another, beaming into the camera as they frolic through a field, swim in the ocean, or squeal in delight as rollercoasters roar to new heights. Many parents have an expectation that a family vacation will be filled with non-stop joy and wonder why the reality rarely lives up to the hyped expectation. Vacations provide a change in routine and amount of structure, as well as exposure to new experiences. For some, this is exciting and provides a much-needed respite from day-to-day schedules. For others, the variation in routine raises anxiety and stress. For many of us, both are true—we look forward to a new experience and also feel anxious about the unknown.

Holidays are also laden with explicit and implicit expectations. Certain foods must appear. Family members return to fixed roles. Gatherings can be simultaneously wonderful and stressful, as everybody has their own agenda and sense of how the holiday should be celebrated. Adherence to strict expectations can often lead to disappointment.

Children who need routines and structure to make sense of the world around them often find the less structured nature of vacations stressful. They also struggle with adhering to the established norms for holiday gatherings; they may be required to participate in traditions that do not appeal to them, with larger groups than they are accustomed to. How do we help our children participate in as well as enjoy family celebrations and vacations? How do we set the stage for success?

Within this chapter you will learn:

- why vacations and holidays are challenging for your child:
  - changes to routine
  - increased social interactions
  - traveling with teens
- strategies to help your family manage vacation glitches:
  - taking transportation
  - choosing a destination
  - balancing divergent needs and interests
- strategies to help your family participate in holiday celebrations:
  - clarifying expectations
  - developing traditions that work for everyone
  - providing options.

## When expectations get in the way of reality

Colleen, mom of 8-year-old Aidan, came to the topic night confused about why vacations were so exasperating and wondering how other parents were managing.

"Our last vacation was so frustrating," Colleen began. "We were going to historic sites and museums in Washington, DC. We let our children each pick one site to go to, and then we took turns at each one. Aidan's pick was the Air and Space Museum. We had been to the other sites his brother and sister chose earlier in the vacation and now it was his turn. But when we finally got there and we had to wait in a short line, Aidan fell apart."

"Mom, I want to go in now. I need to go in now!" Aidan started yelling. Everyone was looking at us and then looking away.

"Aidan, we will go in," Colleen said in a quiet voice. "There are ten people in front of us, and we need to wait our turn. It won't be long."

"No, I need to go in now," Aidan screamed. "It's not fair that I have to wait." Now people were actively backing away.

Colleen didn't know what to do. She just wanted to have an enjoyable holiday with her family.

## Why are vacations and holidays so stressful?

- *Change*: We are taking our children out of their normal routine and asking them to manage in a new setting, with new activities and new people. None of that is easy when you use routines and familiar people to help make sense of the larger world.

- *Demands*: Vacations require compromise and flexibility. Although we can make a plan for vacations, inevitably, some aspect of our time away from home will go differently than we anticipated. When the inevitable glitches occur, our children may not have the extra patience or tolerance required to manage.

- *Increased togetherness*: Many children with Asperger's need time alone to lower the strain they can feel from having to participate in demanding social interactions. Vacations often mean more time together in a smaller space. If our children don't get to alleviate their anxiety, triggers will easily set them off.

- *Social expectations*: Vacations are often spent in public settings surrounded by unfamiliar people. Although parents and siblings will recognize the social norms of the new environments, our children with Asperger's may not. Parents may feel more pressure for their child to fit behaviorally. When parents let the pressure to conform overtake their own understanding of their child's capabilities at that moment in time, their stress and anxiety may overflow onto their child.

- *Developmental delay*: Children with Asperger's are delayed in their development of social-emotional and social-pragmatic skills. When parents vacation where children's activities are divided by age range, they may find that their child does not fit well in their chronological age category. A mismatch of activity and child's interest or abilities leads to stress and frustration.

- *Large social gatherings*: Often at holiday time, extended families gather. Even if children are in their own home to celebrate a holiday, a variety of family members or friends are in attendance as well. Some children with Asperger's find large gatherings of people, even people they know, overwhelming. Additional expectations for social interactions may also raise anxiety.

So does this mean that vacations and holiday gatherings are doomed to fail? Should we just give up, stay home, and let our children do exactly as they please? We don't have to take such extreme measures, although it may feel as if we should just cocoon at home to avoid the additional stressors. Our children need exposure to and practice with handling travel and larger family gatherings. Going to either extreme—vacationing with no accommodation for your child or boycotting opportunities away from home—is unhealthy and unhelpful. Finding the correct balance between exposure to new experiences with the support and structure needed to keep anxiety and stress at a manageable level is crucial. Skills our children demonstrate at home may not make an appearance on vacation or while staying with relatives. Your child isn't trying to make your life difficult; he's struggling with increased demands.

## Traveling with teens

Certain developmental stages can be particularly challenging in their own right. Layer Asperger's on top of adolescence, and you and your child get a double dose of inflexibility. Getting cooperation from your teen when traveling can be difficult. Our family experienced the highs and lows of this a few years back as we ventured out for a weekend away. We found a place where we could all find things we liked to do and bring the dog. We didn't think this would be a contentious issue, but that's where we guessed incorrectly. When we raised the issue with our kids, this was the response given back to us by our newly minted 15-year-old.

"Mom, I don't want to go to New Hampshire for the weekend," Noah said. "If we have to go away, I want to go to New Jersey to visit my friends I haven't seen all year. You need to take me to New Jersey. It's not fair that we're going somewhere new when we haven't gone back to New Jersey like you promised."

"Noah, we will go to New Jersey," I replied. "But for this weekend we're going to New Hampshire."

"I'm a teenager," he said. "My family sucks. I don't want to be with you. The only good thing is that the dog is coming."

For quite a few years, my son had been willing to try new things, travel to new places, eat at new restaurants, and take part in new activities. His flexibility had actually increased, and I didn't have to preview every activity so that he would know what was going to happen. For most of his childhood, I made up schedules, showed him websites, made lists of possible activities, and showed him his choices if he wasn't able to participate or just needed a break. I'd forgotten that he had entered a new developmental phase and that the flexibility he'd shown for many years might be replaced by a less accommodating nature.

HELPFUL POINTS TO REMEMBER WHEN TRAVELING WITH TEENS

- *Don't engage in battle*: Many teens secure your attention and interaction by pushing buttons. All teens have strong and at times overwhelming emotions. Teens with Asperger's have a difficult time managing their strong emotions. Since your teen probably can't control his response in the moment, you need to stay calm and walk away from arguments. Give your teen time to calm down as well.

- *Validate their experience*: Our teens often feel that no one understands them. Letting them know that other teens feel the same way may help. You can also tell them that you heard their concerns and will do your best to address them, however not every disagreement is negotiable.

- *Be flexible*: Decide which activities are negotiable and which are not. Give your teen options for participation when you can.

- *Bring an ally*: Consider bringing pets or friends on vacation with you if possible.

- *Give notice*: If you are expecting them to go with you to particular places or events, give notice ahead of time. Teens don't like to be surprised by what you expect of them. Teens with Asperger's? Even less so.

- *Use humor*: As my kids were entering the teen years, my friend and colleague Robin Lurie-Meyerkopf shared how she and her teens had "forced family fun." Don't try and tell your children how to feel regarding a change that doesn't appeal to them. Humor may help defuse their snarky attitude.

### What to do when vacations seem to take a nose-dive

Let's revisit my family's trip to New Hampshire. Although Noah had enjoyed parts of the weekend, he mostly kept up the constant complaints and seemed resistant to reason.

"Mom, when are we leaving?" he asked. "You said we were going to leave after lunch and archery. I want to leave by 1:30."

"Archery doesn't start until 1:30," I replied. "I don't know exactly when we're leaving, but we'll be home by dinner."

"I need to know when we're leaving," he spat back at me. "I need to know how much time I need to spend in this hellhole."

This is the same person who declared at lunch he was enjoying himself and could imagine coming back again. At this point, I'm starting to feel as if I don't know which child I'm going to get. Noah can be flexible, calm, and mature. This weekend was also highlighting his ability to channel a tantruming 2-year-old through the body of a young man. As we left archery, Noah continued his litany of woes.

"I'm bored," he complained. "I don't have anything to do. I want to go home."

"Noah, it was hot during archery," I explained. "We're going swimming before we head home." "I don't want to go swimming," he declared. "I want to go home NOW. What's it going to take for you to f-ing understand that? Are you a moron?"

I have to admit, by this point in the weekend, my nerves were shot and my reserve of patience had dried up. The weekend I envisioned was not materializing. I felt myself at breaking point as I turned to Noah on the path.

"Noah, I'm not the type of parent who would ever hit her children to teach them a lesson," I said slowly and clearly. "But if I were, I'd be hitting you right now."

Noah went to open his month in response. He closed it again without uttering a word.

"We are going to finish this walk in silence," I said through clenched teeth. "I am not capable of having any constructive conversation right now. I have reached my limit. We will talk about this later."

"But I'm bored," Noah said as we reached the car. "I don't know what to do."

"You can come swim with us to cool off," I offered. "You can sit in the car with the dog and read. You can listen to music. I'm going swimming with your younger brothers. We'll probably be about 30 minutes. You decide which you want to do."

"I don't want to do any of it," Noah replied. "I just want to go."

"Okay, choose the one which is least objectionable," I said. "I'm going swimming at the pool with your brothers. See you in half an hour."

I could see the smoke rising from his forehead. He was agitated. He was frustrated. He wanted everyone to do what he wanted. He needed time alone to calm down. I left him in charge of the dog.

## Repairing relationships

Thirty minutes later we reconvened. I offered beverages and snacks for the ride home and everyone seemed in better spirits. Noah seemed much more content now that we were heading back toward Boston. I, on the other hand, had contemplated my worth as a parent. Someone else had to be better at this than I was. Someone else would have lovingly handled all these situations and understood how to soothe the savage beast that inhabited my child. On the way home, when the stress and agitation levels had dropped, I started to process the weekend with Noah and apologized for my own role in making it worse.

"Noah, I'm sorry that things didn't go as you had hoped this weekend," I said. "I know it was hard for you to come to New Hampshire instead of New Jersey. You are right that we haven't been back in awhile and I can understand how frustrating that might feel. When we're back I can check with our friends and see when they are free for a visit. Does that help?"

"Yeah," Noah replied calmly. "You never talked to me about New Hampshire. When we go away for the weekend, we go to New Jersey. It was a big surprise and I don't like to be surprised."

"I apologize for surprising you," I replied. "But, even if you don't like the surprise, I'd like you to try to talk with me calmly about it. I didn't arrange this trip to upset you. I thought it would be fun for you too. Maybe before we plan another trip, we can work together to find a place that works for everyone. Would you help me with that?"

"I can help with that," he said.

"I'm also sorry I lost my temper with you," I apologized. "I had definitely reached my breaking point. I wanted to enjoy my time with you and the rest of the family. But the continuous complaining and swearing wore me down."

"I was angry," Noah explained as if it weren't clear. "I didn't want to be there."

"I understand that," I said. "But what could you do differently next time you feel that way? All your complaining didn't change the fact that we stayed and it just made us all more miserable. Do you need help figuring out what you could do instead of constantly complaining?"

"I could take a walk with the dog," he suggested.

"That's a good idea," I replied. "It usually helps to have a few ideas for how to calm down. I know you like to listen to music or read. I know you felt crummy, but let's both try and find ways to stay calm when situations feel overwhelming. It can happen to anyone."

"Okay."

All families can struggle with how to handle unstructured time and changes in routine. But families that include children with Asperger's have to address the anxiety and stress their kids experience when changes occur and situations require flexibility. What could I have done differently to help the weekend run more smoothly?

## Strategies to plan your vacation

- *Preview the vacation*: Talk with your child about what you are doing and where you are going. If they like to research information, have them do a web search or look up information you need. Show them what the space looks like and what types of options they will have. Don't assume they can go with the flow in a new situation.

- *Provide some structure*: Clarify timelines for activities. You can offer actual times or let your child know the order of activities; for example, "After lunch, we go swimming." If your child does well with visual schedules, have him help you set the order of activities. As with any schedule, make sure that you let your child know that the activities are subject to change with little notice because circumstances may change.

- *Offer choices*: When you travel with a group, whether it is your own family or friends, compromise is crucial. If there are a few activities or events everyone needs to attend, make that explicit. When you can offer a choice as to which activities to do, let your children choose and make sure each family members get a chance to do what they are most interested in.

- *Help kids wait or have a "Plan B"*: Sometimes on vacation, you will have to wait for someone. Have a list of activities children can do while they wait. This might include reading, listening to music, jumping, running, screen time, or playing cards. Waiting is challenging for kids with Asperger's—they need to know what they can do while they wait.

- *Provide downtime activities*: Sometimes we don't build in enough time for kids to be alone or relax to counteract new activities. Create a list of relaxing alternatives they will be able to do by themselves, or with other family members or friends. This might include watching a movie or show, reading, playing a board or card game, playing or listening to music, and cooking or eating a favorite meal. It's important to remember that our children may need more time to themselves or time away from new activities. We are asking them to stretch their abilities and we also need to provide some respite for all; every moment of vacation does not need to be optimized.

### Transportation travel woes

Let's return to our parent topic night and hear from Claudia.

"To be with my family for the holidays, we have a four-hour car ride. I dread it each time we make the trip. My 10-year-old, Angie, has Asperger's and she hates to be in the car. She just wants to watch videos, but if she does that for too long, she doesn't feel well. If we suggest she do something else, she'll start screaming at us. Then her younger brother, Kevin, will start crying. By the time we've arrived we're all worn out. I don't know what to do."

Allen, dad to 11-year-old Scott, added his own struggle with security at the airport. "We got to the airport two hours before our flight and had to wait in long lines and that's where the trouble started."

"I need to go to the bathroom," Scott said.

"You have to wait right now," Allen responded. "We're in line to check in."

"I can't," Scott said. "I need to go now."

"If we leave the line now, we have to go to the very end and we might miss our flight," Allen explained. "Can you wait until we get through the line? I'll take you as soon as we're done."

"No," Scott responded loudly. "I need to go now. I'm going to have an accident."

"Scott, please, I know you can do this," Allen requested. "Just wait a few minutes, and I will take you."

"I will blow up this place if you don't take me!" Scott yelled.

"I looked up to see passengers and airline personnel staring at us. I tried to tell everyone that my son was just upset and didn't know what he was saying. I explained my son's disability to airport security. After a few questions and a bathroom break, we were allowed on the plane. Throughout the whole process Scott was completely unaware of how his actions impacted our travel plans. I want to travel with him, but now I'm spooked that he'll make this type of comment in public and get in trouble. How do I help him?"

TRANSPORTATION TRAVEL STRATEGIES

- *Preview*: Show your child maps and let them see the travel route. You can use Social Stories™ that explain the traveling process (Gray 2010). The following types of information are helpful to preview:

  - getting ready to go

  - getting to the airport or train station

  - packing the car for a long trip

  - travel delays and what to do while you wait

  - security checkpoints

  - snacks and meals

  - activities you can do while traveling

  - how to stay calm when problems arise.

- *Teach hidden curriculum* (Myles *et al.* 2004): Show your child information on airport security so that he knows what to expect. It's important to talk about what words should not be used at the airport so that he doesn't get in trouble inadvertently.

- *Share the perspective of fellow travelers*: It can be helpful to share how other passengers might be thinking or feeling. For example, if your child is frustrated with waiting, you can let him know that other people feel the same way. It helps your child to begin to build the understanding that he is not the only one who feels a certain way.

- *Provide access to food*: We all can get cranky when our blood sugar dips from lack of food. Pack snack bags for children so that they can easily access an item when needed.

- *Discuss delays*: Travel is filled with delays—waiting in lines, equipment repairs, weather-related slow downs, or traffic delays from construction or accidents. Let your child know in advance that waiting is part of travel, and plan what they can do while they wait. Let them know that the time required to travel may change if extended delays occur.

- *Plan activities*: Your child needs to have some activities to occupy her attention while she is waiting or traveling. Create a list of things she can do independently as well as some ideas for things she can do with a sibling or parent. Depending on the age of your child and her interests some of the following choices may work:

  - books

  - music

  - audio books

  - Mad Libs

  - puzzles (crosswords, sudoku, word search, mazes)

  - screen time

  - card games

  - action figures or dolls

  - fidgets.

- *Take breaks*: If you are traveling by car, build in breaks to get out and move around. Even if children are happily glued to electronics, they still need to move every few hours. If on a train, plane, or bus, make sure to get up and walk the aisle during the trip as well.

- *Distract*: If your child is getting agitated or frustrated, have calming items readily available. For some, it might be as simple as chewing gum or having a sour candy. For others it might be asking them questions about their special interest. It's helpful to have a few ideas ahead of time in case your child needs extra help dealing with the demands of travel.

## Travel destinations—where to go and what to do

At the parent topic night, Danielle, mom of 6-year-old Trevor and 12-year-old Troy talked about how her family feels as if their vacations are held hostage by Trevor's special interests.

"Trevor is happiest in water and can stay in the pool or lake all day. Everyone else wants to do other things, like go to an amusement park or arcade, but Trevor hates rollercoasters and the arcade is too noisy for him. I feel like we need to take separate vacations to make everyone happy, but I want to be with my whole family." What can we do when the interests and needs of family members diverge?

STRATEGIES FOR ASPERGER'S FRIENDLY TRAVEL DESTINATIONS

- *Choose destinations wisely*: Think about the types of places that offer enough variety that everyone in the family can find something they will enjoy. If you are planning a trip with extended family, talk with them about finding the right space to meet the needs of all the people attending. If a destination will be demanding for your child, bring a variety of activities and supports to help him manage challenging situations.

- *Clarify available activities*: Have your children develop a list of possible activities on vacation. Clarify how everybody will have a chance to do their preferred activities. This may help them with participating in or waiting during events that aren't preferred.

- *Make the implicit explicit*: Be clear with your family about how vacations work. Set realistic expectations by pointing out the need to compromise and be flexible. Show your child how her needs will be met and how she can help other family members get what they need too.

- *Be flexible*: If you have enough adult support, you can be flexible about who goes on vacation together and how you spend your time together while away from home. Don't assume that all family members need to do all activities together. Sometimes a little separation, whether on different vacations or doing different activities while traveling together, makes for happier travelers.

- *Expand comfort zones*: Before leaving home, discuss what one new thing each family member will try on vacation. Including the whole family shows that this is not just about your child with Asperger's. The one new thing could be trying a new food, sleeping on the floor in a sleeping bag, or going on a walking tour. Setting the expectation ahead of time clarifies how much and how often your child will need to reach outside her comfort zone.

## Holiday celebrations and expectations

Regardless of whether we are carrying out the longstanding traditions of the family we grew up with or are starting new customs, we bring our expectations for the celebration with us. Try to build in a reality check. Ask yourself the following:

- Have I set realistic expectations?

- Is my child capable of what I am asking him to do?

- Have I considered the stress or anxiety this type of celebration may cause?

- How can I help my child participate in a way that makes sense for her?

- What part of the celebration will be engaging and fun for my child?

- What can my child do if he needs to take a break?

Even though I know what to do, I still have an emotional reaction to the type of celebration I want to offer to my family for our holidays. Especially now, when my son has become capable of so many things, I easily forget that certain situations raise his anxiety and bring out strong reactions. Sometimes his strong reaction catches me off-guard, like it did one year at our Passover Seder.

Noah sat down at the Seder with clenched teeth and rocked in his chair. His face was already red and he looked as if he was in pain. I hoped the discussion we had the previous night would help him get through the evening with our extended family—I'd raised the issue of the Seder the next night as we all sat together.

"Tomorrow night at the Seder I'm hoping you all can be calm, participate, and be nice to each other," I said. "No brothers bickering at the table please."

"Talk to my brothers about that," Noah replied. "They make it so silly. I want to have a more serious discussion at the Seder, and they wreck it. I won't be able to stay calm if they get silly."

"Well, I can't promise your brothers or other people won't be silly at times," I replied. "Seders are filled with discussions and stories and songs; some serious and some lighthearted. What do you think you can do to help yourself stay calm if people do something you don't like?"

"I can bash their head against a wall," Noah offered without a smile and a bit of tone.

"Try again," I volley back to him.

"I don't know," he said. "I could tell them they are idiots."

"How about if you get frustrated by something you excuse yourself from the table or ask your dad or me to help you?" I suggested. "I'm thinking that might work better than physical or verbal abuse of siblings or guests."

"I can try," he offered.

I thought the discussion went well. Noah expressed his intense dislike of certain aspects of the Seder, and we talked about options for handling his strong emotions. But the following night, the Seder quickly deteriorated. Whenever a guest raised a question, Noah responded by diminishing the person instead of discussing the issue. We knew that some of this was from his discomfort and let it go. As the evening wore on, we'd had enough.

"My brothers are idiots," Noah said in a stage whisper.

"Noah, if you need to leave the table because you're feeling bothered, you can," I reminded him.

"I don't want to leave," Noah said loudly. "I want my stupid brothers to leave."

"Your brothers are fine," I said in clipped tones. "But you are not and you can leave if you need to."

We began to sing and Noah covered his ears and yelled, "Why do we have to sing this stupid song?"

"Noah, leave the table," I replied sternly. "The rest of us want to celebrate and sing. You need to leave now."

Noah stared straight at me as he slid back from the table, "What did I do?" he asked completely unaware in the moment of how disruptive he was.

"Just leave," I answered. "I'll talk with you later."

After the Seder, Noah agreed to speak privately with me.

"Noah, do you know what happened tonight?" I asked quietly.

"Sitting with a big group makes me uncomfortable," he said. "I was really grumpy and overly sensitive."

"You really hurt my feelings tonight," I shared. "I like a Seder with a lot of discussion and I encourage all of you to express your opinions. But a lot of your commentary was filled with negative statements about people who were here tonight."

"I was kidding," he replied. "Everyone knew I was kidding. Can't anyone take a joke?" Noah asked as he paced.

"Noah there is a big difference between teasing family members in a good-natured way and saying cruel things with a smile," I explained. "The things you said were mean-spirited and not funny. You may not have intended to hurt others, but the types of comments you made can damage relationships."

"Now who is being too sensitive?" Noah snorted.

"Noah, I know you are a good person who cares about other people," I reassured him. "I also know you can have days like this one, where being with everyone is overwhelming and you say and do things that make you look like you don't care about others. But I'm worried that people will only think of you as a mean-spirited person. They won't take the time to see that you can be kind and helpful, caring and supportive, interesting and creative. All they will see is your vehemence and won't give you a second chance. I can understand how you think I'm overreacting; but what I'm really reacting to is imagining how others will interpret your comments and then label you in a negative light."

"I'm going for a walk," Noah replied as he headed toward the door. I let him go, knowing this was a longer conversation and he was done with it for now. I had made things harder for Noah by pushing him to conform during the evening. If I'd distracted him or used humor, chances were his intense feelings would have dissipated with a smile. I felt hollow inside, but realized I needed to let the expectations for the evening go. He hadn't acted out on purpose; he felt anxious and uneasy in his skin and didn't know how to make those feelings go away or express them in a gentler way.

## Strategies for helping with holidays

- *Realistic expectations*: It is easy to set expectations too high. Think about what will work for your child and family. Don't get swayed into providing a celebration that will set people on edge. Think about what has worked well in the past and what has caused problems. If you are going to be at someone else's home, talk with them about how they are structuring the event and offer to provide items or activities that will help your child manage.

- *Find balance*: Our children need exposure to new situations, so that they can practice being flexible, as well as support to manage the additional stresses these situations bring. We do not need to protect them from all change or social demands that are challenging. We also do not need to provide so many accommodations that we are doing everything for them. When considering holiday events, try to find the right amount of challenge.

- *Designate roles*: Our children often have a difficult time with the open-ended nature of social events. When people are just talking with each other, but the topic isn't of interest, our kids might not know what to do. Let them know a specific role they can play at the event to help them know what to do. It can also help if you ask others in the family to take on roles too. For example, an older cousin can play cards with your child. If you need help to engage your child in a positive interaction, you may need to ask directly.

- *Be flexible*: Think carefully about what structure and events will work for the needs of your family. If an event seems too far outside their ability or comfort zone, have other options so that they can still be part of the group, but don't have to participate in exactly the same way.

- *Provide accommodations*: At a recent holiday celebration at our house, I had Noah brainstorm what he might do to handle the large group of people at our home. He was able to offer two helpful options (sit at the end of the table to have more space and take short breaks away from the large group). He was much more comfortable and able to fully participate in the celebration with those accommodations in place. Think about what types of supports you can offer to help children feel at ease.

## Setting panic aside

Travel, unstructured time, and holiday celebrations can be exciting, anxiety producing, refreshing, and stressful all at once. To help our children manage challenges, think about what they need and what they are capable of, then provide just the right amount of support without taking away the opportunity for them to expand their abilities. Keep your expectations realistic and bring your sense of humor with you!

# CHAPTER 9

# Chronic Stress

*Building a Balanced Life*

Unrealistic expectations cause stress. Sometimes we can lower the amount of stress we face by changing our exposure to demanding situations or people. But when we can't eliminate or avoid the source of tension, we need to find ways to cope so that it doesn't create chronic mental and physical health concerns or lead to collateral damage in relationships.

As parents of children on the autism spectrum, we face additional stressors. We receive conflicting information regarding the efficacy of intervention approaches. Usually, therapies require extensive time and money. How do we know if any of them will help our children forge connections and remediate challenges? We can't place our children in isolation, providing one intervention at a time and removing all others. How can we be certain which one will lead to positive change? This sense of the unknown causes strain as we try to untangle the available information and claims so we can make informed decisions on our child's behalf.

We feel stress when our children suffer. We worry when our hopes for our children are in direct opposition to their own wishes or abilities. The on-going unknowns can keep us on high alert. We try to acknowledge and accept our children for who they are in this moment while simultaneously examining what intervention or support might help them. But how do we manage this amplified state of vigilance so that it doesn't completely overwhelm us? We have to throw away the yardstick to relieve the pressure to "catch up" (Drezner 2012). We have to find ways to manage the stress so that it doesn't take over.

Throughout this chapter on chronic stress, you will learn about:

- sources and consequences of chronic stress:
  - unrealistic or differing expectations between parents
  - Groundhog Day syndrome
  - triggers
- suggestions for managing chronic stress:
  - setting realistic expectations
  - connecting to others
  - accessing help
- developing a balanced approach:
  - how much is enough?
  - prioritizing
  - infrastructure maintenance.

## Sources and consequences of chronic stress

*Unrealistic or differing expectations*

For years I wanted Jed to be as knowledgeable about Asperger's as I was. I wanted him to read everything I read, search the websites I recommended, and review the highlighted articles I left him. One night we were talking about my wish that he would invest the time to learn about Asperger's.

"I don't understand why you don't read the books and articles I leave for you," I said. "Don't you want to know more about Asperger's?"

"Is there something in particular you want me to read so we can discuss it?" he asked. "Do you want my opinion on something you're thinking about or do you just want me to be better informed in general?"

"I want you to care about this as much as I do," I answered, my voice rising. "I feel like you expect me to do all the work. But what if I miss something? There's no way I can do this all on my own. I need your help to keep up."

"I'm not sure reading more will make me helpful," he explained. "I won't ever know as much as you do when it comes to Asperger's or autism. It's your profession, how can I match that?"

"You don't have to match it," I clarified. "But I want you to feel the need to learn more. I want you to seek out the information, or at least review the information I bring to you. Right now I feel like I'm doing this all on my own."

"You aren't alone in this," Jed answered calmly. "I want the same things you do for our kids and for us. But I can't be you. I think you want me to feel and act the same way you do when it comes to anything having to do with our kids and Asperger's. I want to help, but I'm not you and I can't be your clone. We have to figure out how I can support you without needing to be a carbon copy of you."

We sat silently for a few moments and then it dawned on me, "Oh crap—he's right."

I realized that I hadn't been feeling supported by Jed because he didn't tend to initiate any discussion about Asperger's or seek out more information. But as he had tried to tell me many times before, he felt as if he had to focus on and address professional frustrations. If he lost his job, our family would lose its financial security. That's what kept him awake at night. He didn't have any room left for feeling anxious or unsure about Asperger's because he knew I would handle whatever challenges arose. Like many parents, we had different expectations that led to incorrect assumptions.

WHY DO DIFFERING EXPECTATIONS RAISE OUR STRESS LEVELS?

- *Polarizing points of view*: When we are under the hold of chronic stress, we don't offer our most flexible and accommodating selves. We tend to seek out information or feelings that support our beliefs and ignore data that might poke even the smallest hole in our perspective. We end up painting ourselves into a dogmatic corner when we allow being right to be more important than resolving our dilemma.

- *Mind reading*: Parents often get in trouble because they expect their partner to read their mind. They may think that their spouse should know how they feel, what they think and what they expect. Presuming our partner will intuit our expectations regarding our children often leads to disappointment.

- *False assumptions*: When those close to us act in ways we don't expect, we may assume that they don't care or find our concern inconsequential or unimportant.

- *Brewing resentments*: When we face chronic stress over unresolved and long-term predicaments, we can start to harbor resentments over anyone or anything that doesn't aid in the resolution.

Let's revisit our conversation and see if we can find a way to address our out-of-sync expectations.

"Jed, I may have wanted you to be me, but we both know that two of me is not a good idea," I ventured. "What I really want is for you to share some of the anxiety and burden I feel with managing all the kids' needs. I need support."

"Okay, but you have to be specific," Jed replied. "You can't just say I need to do more or that I need to care more about it. I care about it, but I can't help that I need to put almost all of my mental energy toward work. If you give me something specific, I will do it."

"All right, let's set a time to figure this out," I said. "Maybe we can start by attending team meetings together."

Although this conversation went fairly smoothly and resulted in positive changes, many of our previous conversations did not. When expectations diverge or aren't realistic, what can you do to lower your stress level?

### MANAGING STRESS BY SETTING REALISTIC EXPECTATIONS

- *Set aside time to discuss your expectations*: It is challenging to find time to have a whole conversation without interruption when you're a parent. You may need to set an appointment with your spouse or partner so that you can talk honestly about your expectations.

- *Leave other issues out of the discussion*: It's very easy to start a conversation about one topic (like your expectations for help with a school team) and end up bringing up other disagreements and unmet hopes in your relationship. Although you may have valid points, it's best to stick to the specific issue you are trying to resolve. Pointing out other long-lasting predicaments lessens the chance you will resolve the issue at hand.

- *Check your expectations*: Whether the expectations are for yourself, your partner or spouse, or your children, it can be helpful to get a second opinion. Sometimes a knowledgeable and unemotionally attached ally can help you see which expectations seem realistic and which might not.

- *Be kind*: Parenting is hard. There is always more to do and no way to get it all done. It helps to remember that you are on the same team, working to figure out what your children need and prioritizing what needs to get addressed. Don't be too hard on yourself or those around you. Everyone faces unresolved challenges. We need to be patient with ourselves and others when things don't go as planned.

### Groundhog Day syndrome

In the movie *Groundhog Day*, Bill Murray plays a TV weathercaster who wakes each morning to relive Groundhog Day over and over again. At a recent parent topic night on chronic stress, Marissa, mom of 10-year-old Harry, commented on how she feels as if she is stuck, like Bill Murray, each fall when she meets with her school team.

"At the end of every school year we meet with Harry's team to create a smooth transition with next year's teacher," Marissa said. "But when the new school year begins, Harry struggles for the first two months. When we meet with his team in the fall, it's the same conversation we've had all the previous falls. Even though the teachers change, the dialogue remains the same. This is what happened at our meeting last month."

"Harry is coming home frustrated," Marissa explained to the team. "He says that the teacher isn't letting him take breaks or chew gum in class. These things really help him pay attention and stay calm. Could you tell us what's happening?"

"I know that's what he used last year," the new teacher explained in a calming voice. "But before we assume he'll need that much support, I like to see what he can do without it. He might be more capable than we think."

"The wait and see approach is applied each fall and we always need to add the supports back in," Marissa explained in an exasperated voice. "Meanwhile Harry struggles through the first two months of school confused and frustrated. The other kids notice he can't manage. Are we waiting for him to refuse to come to school before providing the accommodations and supports we agreed on at the end of last year?"

"If he needs them, he will get them," his teacher replied. "But I'm not sure he needs them. If he just tried a bit harder he would be fine."

"At that point I excused myself and left the room crying," Marissa explained with slumped shoulders. "I had heard enough. I felt like trying to get the team to implement the accommodation and support plan was a Sisyphean task and each fall we begin at the bottom of the hill after almost reaching the top the previous spring." The parents around the room were nodding in agreement. Why do parents of children on the autism spectrum experience so many Groundhog Day moments?

WHY DO CONTINUED EXPOSURE TO FRUSTRATING
SITUATIONS CAUSE OUR STRESS LEVELS TO RISE?

- *Unmet expectations*: When agreed-upon accommodations and services aren't provided, the team is not delivering what it had already approved. Often it is hard to decipher why an agreed-upon part of the program is not being made available, which can cause resolutions to grind to a halt.

- *Lack of transparency*: Even though school systems may have some well-constructed interventions or programs, not all teachers or schools are aware of available resources. Program development might be too dependent upon specialized knowledge of the few instead of sharing of information for the whole.

- *Lack of communication*: Sometimes your child's teacher doesn't communicate her experience of working with your child to the receiving team. If every fall the new team needs to reinvent the wheel, instead of accessing practical knowledge from trusted colleagues, time is wasted and frustration and stress increase.

- *Lack of expertise*: Sometimes teachers think our children aren't working hard enough. They get labeled as lazy. Teachers might determine that processing challenges and behaviors are character flaws instead of symptoms resulting from unmet needs. It is difficult to dialogue with a teacher who believes that your child is intentionally difficult.

- *Learned helplessness*: When situations are more problematic than they need to be and no one is offering a clear path to smooth out the bumps, parents can begin to feel as if nothing they do will help. Parents may feel emotionally and physically depleted and have little energy left to advocate. The seeds of ineffectiveness and despair can take root, and learned helplessness—the sense that you have no control over your situation—can paralyze parents.

Let's revisit the topic night with Marissa.

"I left the room feeling hopeless," she continued. "I mean what does it take to get people to do what they promise to do? I think the teachers are good people who believe they are doing the right thing, but they're ignoring the seasoned expertise of the teachers who have already worked with him. I'm so worn out from having this same discussion every fall. When will it stop?"

Marissa is wondering how she can resolve the problem—a problem that she believes should not have existed in the first place. She may be right, but here she is dealing with it again. Not only does she need to address the present concern, but she also needs to manage her deep frustration and sense of despair brought on by the on-going stress.

### WHAT CAN PARENTS DO WHEN THEY ARE FACED WITH REPETITIVE PROBLEMS AND FEEL COMPLETELY WORN DOWN BY THEM?

- *Put requests in writing*: If you seem to have the same conversations with your child's educational team, but nothing gets resolved or answered explicitly, put your requests in writing and request a response within a reasonable time frame.

- *Know your child's rights*: Depending on where you live, you will have different national and local laws that regulate special education. For example, in the United States, your child's Individualized Education Plan (IEP) specifies what services, supports, and accommodations are provided. No team member can decide individually that a service is no longer needed and stop providing it without consulting the team and amending the IEP. You can request that your child's team "reconvenes" in order to discuss any needed changes to a program or placement and amend the IEP.

- *Talk with other parents*: It helps to talk with parents who have similar experiences. You can also learn what has worked for them. You can learn what types of requests are reasonable and more likely to be implemented.

- *Access support*: In addition to talking with other parents, parents can contact organizations or professionals who can offer information, support, consultation, training, and validation. AANE serves as a lifeline for parents when they face these dilemmas.

- *Recognize what you have control over*: When you are faced with long-term problems, it can feel as if nothing can change and that you are held hostage by indecision and delay. Consider what you can do and what is beyond your control. For the pieces of the problem you can impact, make a plan for how to approach the task. Contemplate how you can manage your frustration or anxiety over what is out of your control. Obsessing over the components of a problem that are not in your power to change causes excessive stress.

## Triggers

Let's rejoin the parent topic night on chronic stress and hear from Diane, mom of 13-year-old Cody.

"My problem is that I seem to blow up over small things," Diane began. "But it's the same small things. I was with my family for the weekend and I lost my temper with my step-dad Walter. He's a wonderful man and I know he cares about Cody, but I couldn't hear his recommendations one more time. We definitely got off on the wrong foot. It started after a rainy afternoon Cody spent playing computer games."

"Diane, Cody is on his computer a lot," Walter said. "He doesn't seem to move around very much. Don't you think it would be good for him to get some exercise?"

Diane sighed heavily and tried to keep her voice calm, but inside her heart was racing and she wanted to run away from the conversation. "The computer is very calming to him and exercise is hard for him," she explained. "There aren't many physical activities that he can do well. If you want to go for a walk with him that's great, but I can't do one more thing. I'm at my limit."

"I just think exercise would help," Walter replied. "He's getting very large and all the time on the computer makes things worse. I can take him for a walk when the rain stops."

"You can see if he'll go for a walk with you," Diane responded. "But instead of thinking that the computer is the problem, maybe you can try and see it as a tool he uses to calm down."

"Exercise might help him feel better too," Walter continued. "At least I can try while he's here."

"Everyone seems to think they could raise Cody better than I can," Diane explained to the other parents. "It's not that I think I have all the answers, but they don't know what it's like to live with him. I'm doing the best I can. I have to coach him on all the big things other people expect him to know, like how to listen to other people when they talk, how to introduce himself to new people, and all the other social things he struggles with. I don't think people who offer suggestions realize how many different things we are working on and how overwhelming it can be for all of us."

"When Walter made his observation it brought up all the other times people offer suggestions without taking our reality into account," Diane said. "I know he meant well, but it's like a groove has been dug out in my brain and whenever anyone makes a comment on the topic of what we could be doing, it sets off a chain reaction."

Many parents can relate to Diane's reaction. Part of the reason she may have reacted so strongly was because she too had been concerned about Cody's weight gain and lack of exercise. But having Walter point it out to her, when she hadn't been able to address it successfully, was the tipping point. Parents often try to address multiple areas of need simultaneously. When we or our children are overwhelmed, we feel more stressed and become less effective. We also become less able to hear any advice that might be perceived as criticism and may release our frustration on unsuspecting, well-intentioned but misinformed, purveyors of opinion.

### Handling triggers

What can parents do when certain situations or conversations act as triggers? How can they manage their response to the stress triggers cause?

- *Acknowledge your triggers*: The first step is recognizing what your triggers are. Parents aren't always aware what sets them off or why.

- *Anticipate triggers*: Once you know what your triggers are, you can start to anticipate when you might be likely to face them. If you know in advance that they might pull you, you will feel more prepared when they arise.

- *Stay in the present*: Even though people and situations may seem similar, try not to take out your past frustrations on new people or situations. It helps to have an explanation if you do over-react to an innocent mistake. "I'm sorry, it's just hard for me when people offer advice. I know you're trying to be helpful, but it feels as if you're judging me."

- *Calming strategies*: Think through what you will do to regain your sense of control when triggers confront you. Will you take some slow, deep breaths? Will you excuse yourself to take a break from the situation? Will you tell yourself that the person means well, even if what they say is hurtful? Practice using whatever strategies appeal to you so that they become more familiar and easier to use.

## Developing a balanced approach

Lisa, mom of 7-year-old Hannah, looked as if she'd been run over by a bus when she showed up at the topic night on chronic stress.

"I feel completely overwhelmed and incompetent," Lisa began. "I was sitting in the waiting room at the clinic where Hannah just started going for occupational therapy [OT] and I overheard other parents talking."

"Are you going to try 'therapy x'?" the first mom with dark hair asked. "Sarah's OT recommended it for her and I think it's helping."

"Susan, our OT, recommended that and 'intervention y,'" the other mom with short grey hair answered. "I don't know about doing both, but we will probably try one and see if it makes a difference. We love Susan and trust her advice. If she thinks these things will help, we'll try them."

"It's a pain to come for all the extra visits, and the costs really add up, but I'm willing to try anything when I get a strong recommendation from Sarah's OT," the first mom continued. "She must know what she's talking about."

"I agree," the second mom replied enthusiastically. "Susan really thinks our son will drop his diagnosis in the next couple of years because of all the intervention we're doing. If she thinks it's possible, then I'm willing to do anything to lose that label."

Lisa was shaking as she re-told the story. "I'm so confused," she said. "I didn't think my daughter could 'lose' her diagnosis. If more intervention and different types of therapies could help my daughter, why aren't I doing more? How do I know what works and what doesn't? I feel like a terrible mom because I'm not researching what other approaches might help. But I cannot drag my child to one more appointment. She doesn't want it and I already feel overwhelmed by all the things we should be doing. How do I know when we are doing enough?"

Lisa's not alone in her confusion. Parents of children on the autism spectrum are exposed to sales pitches and promises on a regular basis. It is beyond the scope of this book to evaluate any particular therapeutic approach or intervention. But before adding to or replacing your child's intervention or therapies, consider the questions in Table 9.1 to help you develop a balanced therapeutic approach.

**Table 9.1**: Considerations for intervention

| Intervention or therapy | Why are we considering this approach? | Pros and cons of this approach | Do we have the time, money and energy for this approach? | How will we evaluate its effectiveness? How will we know when we are done with it? |
|---|---|---|---|---|
|  |  |  |  |  |
|  |  |  |  |  |

## *How do you know whether you are doing enough?*

- *Shift the question*: Instead of asking whether we are doing enough, we can shift to asking whether we are addressing our priorities. This requires us to think through the areas that bring the greatest concern and challenge and develop plans for how to tackle them.

- *More means more*: We've been trained to think that more intervention and therapy is always better. More therapy just means more therapy. More doesn't always equate with better results. It's most important to think of the quality and focus of intervention first and then consider how much time is required to meet goals. More ineffective intervention will not yield positive outcomes.

- *Balance needs and interests*: No child or family can focus on intervention all the time. It becomes tedious. Building in time for interests is important. Also consider how much time various family members may need to decompress.

- *Consider developmental stage*: At different developmental stages your child may have more ability and interest in formal interventions. If he has been participating positively and then becomes reluctant, it may be time to have a conversation with the interventionist to discuss what may have changed. Consider different models and approaches to teaching and practicing skills as our children grow and develop. What worked at 7 won't work at 17.

- *Consider transitions*: During periods of transition—to a new school or new stage of life—our children will likely need more help. It makes sense to learn about and plan for upcoming transitions, while anticipating the glitches that may occur.

- *Consider time of year*: Many of our children run out of steam as the school year drags on. Sometimes, by early spring they've had enough and can't take on one more new thing. If your child has a pattern of fizzling out when faced with long-term demands, consider giving more free time, more support, or cutting out draining activities during times when stamina is low.

- *Consider parental stamina*: Kathryn Collins-Wooley, parent and psychologist in Massachusetts, points out that parents have seasons of depletion too. Recognize when you may need time to decompress or replenish your internal resources. Just as your child's stamina ebbs and flows, yours will too.

- *Recognize what is good enough*: Give yourself credit for doing the best you can with what you know at any given point in time. Over time, your sense of what your child needs and how to meet those needs, will change. Feelings of urgency to "fix what is broken" are often replaced by a desire to help our children feel comfortable with who they are and learn how Asperger's affects them. Helping your child learn how to understand herself, compensate for challenges, and build on strengths works throughout the lifespan.

- *Recognize what is good for your family life*: Parents often feel pressure to keep increasing therapies, even when travel time and attendance make it hard for families to feel as if they have good quality of life. Collins-Wooley asks us to remember that time spent with family members your child enjoys—playing games together, sharing a meal, watching a favorite show, volunteering, or being silly together—reinforce positive connections for all. Allow yourself to set the amount and type of intervention that works for your family.

## Infrastructure maintenance—taking care of yourself so that you have the stamina to care for your family

Let's revisit our topic night on chronic stress and hear from Flora, mom of 15-year-old Stephen.

"My husband is worried about me," Flora explained. "He says I need to take a break because all I think about is Stephen. My son seems sad most of the time. He doesn't talk to anyone outside of school. No one texts or calls him and kids make fun of him on Facebook. He's so innocent and yet he can get into trouble because of what he doesn't know. If I'm not explaining things to him or talking to other people about him, he fails. I don't see any of this changing. I can't take time for myself."

Flora's concern is common. How can she possibly take a break when there is so much to do and nobody else able to do it? We all need respite from the marathon of parenting a child on the spectrum.

IF WE DON'T FIND WAYS TO TAKE CARE OF OURSELVES AS WE CARE FOR OUR CHILDREN, WHAT WILL HAPPEN?

- *Burnout*: Caregivers know this phenomenon well. If we put all our time and energy into caring for others and don't replenish our own resources, our ability to help our children and others will diminish.

- *Resentment*: We can start to feel resentful about the amount of time and energy required. Our feelings may be directed at our child, co-parent, spouse, friends, professionals, and educators.

- *Looping thoughts*: We may start to perseverate on unresolved or complicated problems. We may be unable to think about other people or concerns that need attention.

- *Ineffective problem solving*: When we don't take a break from on-going issues, we can become ineffective and inflexible at solving problems. We may keep trying the same unproductive approaches and expecting a different result.

- *Fear contagion*: When a parent is fearful about her child, it can easily spread to other adults and children. Your home can become "fear central" when you don't manage your own emotional reaction to your child's on-going challenges.

As parents, we are the backbone of the family, making sure everything runs as it needs to. But what if we break down? Collins-Wooley explains that we need to perform infrastructure maintenance so that we can continue to have the stamina to do our jobs. The best way to care for our children is to perform regularly scheduled parental tune-ups so that we don't have massive engine failure.

WHAT DOES INFRASTRUCTURE MAINTENANCE LOOK LIKE?

- *Delegate*: It's important to recognize what responsibilities you can hand over to others. What tasks can you let go of and let someone else manage? Can you teach another person to take over for you? Expanding the network of competency is key to managing stress. Although someone else might complete a task differently, it will still get done and you don't have to do it. Keep the crucial tasks and let the others go. Every few months we have family meetings to assign household jobs. My husband and I have to schedule time to discuss and divide household and childcare responsibilities. We make decisions together so that delegation doesn't become one more task I have to complete.

- *Build in support*: It's hard to manage so many different moving pieces without adequate support. Think of how to divide tasks within your immediate family. What jobs can a partner or spouse, if available, take on? Which jobs can children manage? Look beyond your immediate family and consider how you can reciprocate with friends or extended family to make on-going tasks easier. Consider childcare or housekeeping help if that's within your budget.

- *Distraction*: Find an engaging activity to transport yourself away from your regular concerns. Although we may think we don't have the time to think about or do other activities, we will be more effective and creative if we take some time away. For some, the distraction could be reading a book or watching a movie that isn't about Asperger's or autism. For others it could be joining a group or indulging in a hobby that requires concentration. Collins-Wooley points out the additional benefits of "divided loyalties." When parents have to focus on other people, work, or commitments, they provide their children with mild pressure for independence and help them feel more confident with other caretakers. Divided loyalties may take the form of a job, volunteer commitments, other children, or aging parents.

- *Relaxation*: For some parents, meditation may offer a break from the anxiety and worry that cloud the mind when faced with on-going problems. Meditation practice can provide the opportunity to watch what goes on in our mind without getting caught up in it. It can help us learn to differentiate between noticing a situation or emotional state and getting drawn into it.

- *Physical activity*: Many parents find that physical activity provides an outlet for stress. Determine whether you are more likely to be active if you have an exercise partner or whether you prefer some time to yourself. Start with small goals, like walking ten minutes a day, so that you are more likely to be successful. Imagine how much better you will feel when your physical and mental health is addressed.

- *Fun*: What makes you smile? When do you laugh the hardest? What are your most pleasant memories? When our days are filled with tasks to do, it is easy to let the things that bring us joy fall off our radar.

- *Model healthy habits*: When you take time for infrastructure maintenance, you show your children how you sustain a sense of balance and optimism when faced with on-going demands.

## Setting panic aside

We will always have stress in our lives. But *how* we approach stressful situations can significantly impact how deeply they affect us. Although it can be almost impossible to feel that we can take a break, it's in our children's best interest to invest in our own wellbeing. By taking care of ourselves, we increase our stamina and effectiveness. We also help our children see how to counteract the corrosive effects of on-going stress.

# CHAPTER 10

# Raising Capable and Resilient Kids

What does independence look like for a child or adult with Asperger's? Sometimes it seems as if we expect more from our children with Asperger's than we do from our neurotypical children. We may push them to use skills that are difficult for them, not allowing for typical shifts in energy or ability. Yet if we don't push at all, our children might not interact with others or manage the demands of school, home, and work. How do we know if we need to do more or less?

Although we focus on striving for independence, the reality is that all of us are really *inter*dependent. As adults we need skills that help us interact with others in a variety of settings. Being effectively interdependent is often a challenge for our children. They may not recognize what others need from them or think about how to build relationships to make daily life function with less friction.

It's important to remember that our children are delayed in their social-emotional development, and so the typical timetables need to be adjusted. Parental frustrations diminish when we set aside comparisons and consider our child's abilities and challenges in their own light.

At each developmental stage, we can offer children opportunities to practice everyday problem solving skills independently. In order for our children to have the skills they need to interact positively with others and manage at school, work, and in the community, they need to recognize their own strengths and challenges, and try different ways of solving problems within safe environments.

Throughout this chapter on raising capable and resilient kids, you will learn the importance of:

- building proficiencies throughout childhood and adolescence:
  - independence and interdependence
  - exposure to new experiences in safe environments
  - assessing independence and interdependence capabilities of teens
- helping your child become a problem solver:
  - setting realistic expectations
  - using declarative language
- building resilience:
  - normalizing mistakes
  - focusing on abilities and interests
  - practicing solving problems
  - creating Asperger's/autism spectrum-friendly environments.

## Interdependence and independence

Terri, mom of 10-year-old Sonya, came to our topic night on raising capable kids. She explained her current dilemma with her daughter.

"My husband, Chris, thinks I'm doing too much for Sonya," she began. "He thinks she can do all the things he asks of her without any help. I might be doing too much, but she also can't do all he asks without any support. We both want to do what will help Sonya, but can't seem to agree on how. Here's what happened last week."

"Sonya, we're leaving the house in half an hour for grandma's," Chris yelled toward Sonya's room. "You need to clean your room before we go."

"Sonya didn't respond and Chris didn't go check on her," Terri explained. "I don't know whether she didn't hear him, heard him and ignored him, or didn't know what he expected her to do. But his approach and her lack of response weren't going to produce a happy ending before we left the house."

"Chris showed up at Sonya's bedroom door," Terri continued. "She had clothes all over the floor, and books covered the space clothes didn't. There were wet towels draped over chairs, Lego scattered on top of books, and gum wrappers in her bed. I could see the smoke coming out of Chris's ears."

"Sonya! I told you to clean your room before we left for grandma's a half hour ago," Chris yelled. "You haven't done anything! No screen time tonight. I don't know why you can't just do what we ask you to do!"

"MOM!" Sonya yelled, putting Terri in the middle again.

"Honey, it's okay," Terri said. "I'll help you."

Chris walked away in a huff, "Why do you baby her?" he asked. "She can do this on her own. If you do everything for her, how will she ever learn to do it for herself? Don't you want her to be able to do things without us always showing her over and over again?"

"Of course I want her to learn to do things for herself," Terri replied. "But I think your way just makes her more upset."

What are parents supposed to do when they have the same goal in mind but their approaches and philosophies differ?

## Sowing the seeds for developing independence

- *Parents need to be on the same page*: Parents agree that they would like their children to become more independent. The difficulty comes when they disagree about *how* to help that to occur. There are a variety of ways our children build this capacity. Productive discussion can lead to a coordinated approach. Set time to do the following together:

- Discuss goals for your child.

- Evaluate what has or has not worked in the past.

- Decide which approach you will try.

- Talk about how you will support each other.

- *Consider current capabilities*: Be aware of your child's current ability to accomplish a task. If you ask your child to complete a task they have never done, you may need to provide instruction or coaching as they work through the steps. If your child has been shown how to accomplish the task and still cannot do it, you may need to provide some of the following:

- Break down the task into smaller pieces.

- Provide a visual aid or written list clarifying all the steps.

- Ask questions to help them think through what they need to do to complete the task.

- Be available to help problem solve before frustrations lead to meltdowns.

- *Eliminate all-or-nothing thinking*: Many parents provide intensive support for their children when they are young, hoping they'll grow out of that need. When that scenario doesn't materialize, some parents stop providing help out of frustration or exhaustion. Meeting in the middle, providing instruction or support when needed, as well as providing opportunities to practice taking on more responsibility and problem solving is critical as children get older. Assess your own parenting style and consider whether your approach is skewed too far to one side or the other.

- *Provide learning opportunities at home and out in the community for developing independence*: Our children need to have opportunities to practice jobs so that they can see what works easily for them and where they have more difficulty. To build their sense of competence and resilience, let glitches arise so they can try to resolve them. Before adding new responsibilities, consider what type of support your child may need to accomplish the task she is given. Possible options may include:

  ◦ Ideas for elementary-aged children:

    » cleaning room

    » feeding pet

    » setting and clearing the table

    » putting laundry away in drawers

    » showering/bathing

    » brushing teeth

    » getting dressed.

  ◦ Additional ideas for middle-school-aged pre-teens:

    » helping choose, shop for, and cook meals

    » doing the laundry

    » walking pets

    » choosing the right clothes for the weather

    » keeping track of responsibilities on calendar

    » planning walking and biking routes for excursions

    » ordering and paying for food in a restaurant.

- Additional ideas for high-school-aged teens:
  - » managing money (debit card)
  - » planning excursions with public transportation
  - » personal hygiene—learning how to shave
  - » managing leisure time
  - » building in time for exercise and being active
  - » internships, volunteering, or job (with job coach).

As we're sowing the seeds for developing independence, we need to consider what skills our children need to become more interdependent too.

### Which interdependence proficiencies do our children need to work and play well with others?

- *Social pragmatics*: Using social pragmatics in a dynamic way across a variety of settings and activities with different types of people requires life-long learning. The fast-paced back and forth of social interaction places extraordinary demands on a child who does not process social information intuitively.

- *Executive functioning*: Parents often act as the prosthetic frontal lobes for their child. A child needs to practice using his own frontal lobes and recognize what types of accommodations help him effectively use executive functioning skills.

- *Perspective taking*: Understanding what other people might be thinking and feeling is a critical skill needed to get along with others at home, work, school, and out in the community.

- *Emotional regulation*: Staying calm and coping with frustrations is necessary for adult life; day-to-day glitches will occur, people will be irritating at times, and on-going stressors will exist. No one will tolerate meltdowns on a regular basis from an adult.

- *Flexibility*: Managing social interaction requires flexibility. Being able to accept a different point of view or a different way of accomplishing a task helps our children get along with others.

Penelope, mom to 12-year-old Max, came to the topic night on raising capable kids questioning when her son would be able to use the skills he'd been taught for the past six years. "Max got detention again. He was supposed to be working in a group, and one of the boys in his group knew how to get Max to lose his temper. So Max swore at the other boy and ran out of the school. The other kid didn't get in trouble, but Max did. When will he learn to control his temper? If you talk to Max when he's calm, he seems to know what to do. But when he's confronted with a real-life frustration, it seems like he still goes straight to a big reaction. Can we ever expect him to get better at this?"

Many parents wonder when their children will use the skills they've been taught. How will our children become more interdependent?

## Practical strategies for enhancing interdependence —turning learning into action

- *Interdependence requires effort*: For many people with Asperger's, working with other people is more challenging than working alone. Have patience and understanding for the amount of effort required from your child to work with others.

- *AS-friendly environments*: Our children are more likely to be able to use the skills they have learned if the environment is conducive to practicing what is hard for them, without the threat of punishment. Think about what makes your child feel comfortable and what helps him interact with others. We need to meet our children halfway—we can't expect them to do all the hard work of learning and using interactive skills without us considering how to make their environment AS friendly. Depending on your child you might consider the following:

- include a pet
- include a friend or relative with a positive relationship with your child
- include discussion of a special interest
- use a familiar setting
- offer snacks
- be explicit and include written directions/expectations if applicable
- focus on one or two skills at a time
- keep challenging interactions short to increase the likelihood of success.

- *Dynamic interactions*: Social skills taught in isolation are not sufficient to prepare our children for dynamic social interactions. Drawing their attention to the context around them and pointing out relevant cues may help them consider how to interact (Vermeulen 2012).

- *Provide a mix of learning, practicing, and processing*: The developmental stage of your child and his past experience in social learning will guide your approach to formal and experiential instruction. Think creatively about how your child will be most likely to accept information and feedback while practicing challenging social interactions.

- *Shift responsibilities*: Work with your child to help him find organizational or planning systems that are effective. Some pre-teens and teens prefer using assistive technology (e.g. a calendar on a phone, tablet, or computer to set reminders and plan out work) to track their schedule and responsibilities.

- *Allow glitches and don't rush to solve problems*: When our children face challenges, help them think through options instead of telling them what to do. Glitches provide opportunities for them to practice resolving problems. Resilience comes from facing challenges and figuring them out—even if they don't resolve the way we intended.

- *Change routines occasionally*: Routines and schedules help our children to make sense of the world around them. They are important tools to lower anxiety and smooth transitions. Changes in routine help our children practice being flexible when deviations occur. Providing enough structure so that our children can predict what their day will be like, and infusing small changes to encourage and develop flexibility, offers the right balance.

- *Point out other perspectives*: Be aware of chances to discuss different points of view with your child. Explain perspectives that differ from your child's own. Debate teams or clubs offer the opportunity to learn how to argue opposing positions and think about why others might have different opinions. Public speaking classes also can be useful to expand your child's perspective.

- *Build in self-calming activities*: Create a unique list of options for your child and try to build them into his day. Whether it's doing something active, like karate or running, or something more passive, like reading a book in a quiet space, regular practice will help it become a healthy habit.

## Intelligence and independent living

Audrey, a parent at a recent topic night on raising independent kids, was worried about how her son would manage when he went off to college in the fall. "Jeff has always been really smart," Audrey began. "His teachers love talking to him. He's always got a lot to say about academic subjects. He gets all As and Bs, so the school doesn't think he needs any support. They say he'll do fine when he goes to college. But they don't see how impaired he can look over the simplest things, like taking a shower. I'm always surprised by the types of conversations he and I need to have." Audrey relayed one of her recent interactions with Jeff during breakfast.

"Jeff, did you take a shower?" Audrey asked cautiously.

"Yeah."

"But your hair's not wet," Audrey commented in a neutral tone.

"My regular shampoo wasn't in the shower, so I didn't wash it," Jeff replied.

"I bought new shampoo and put it in the shower," Audrey said. "Did you look at the new bottles that are in there?"

"No," Jeff answered. "If I don't see my regular bottle, I don't wash my hair."

"But what if I buy a different type of shampoo or put it on the other side of the shower?" Audrey asked. "Do you look to see if another bottle will work?"

"No," Jeff answered. "If my shampoo bottle or soap isn't in its regular bottle or in its regular place, I just use the water."

"If you are out of shampoo or soap what do you do?" Audrey asked.

"I just use water," Jeff answered clearly unsure of another option.

"That's one way to handle that situation," Audrey said. "You could also go to the store and buy the shampoo and soap you like. Maybe next time we could go together so that you can see where it is and how much it costs."

"Okay, I guess."

"Until then, if you don't see the shampoo or soap you use in its regular place, will you scan the shower for others you can use?" Audrey asked. "It's okay to use other people's toiletries in our own family. If you are away on a trip or at school, you can only use your own though. Does that make sense?"

"Yep."

Audrey is worried that her teenager won't be able to manage out in the world on his own. Being smart is a fine trait, but it does not equate to having independent living skills when you are on the autism spectrum. How do we ascertain our child's current abilities and challenges for living independently?

## ASSESSING INDEPENDENCE AND INTERDEPENDENCE ABILITIES FOR TEENS

We can't assume that capabilities automatically exist or that our children don't understand what's required of them in the moment. We have to begin by learning about our teen's current awareness and abilities. Beyond having a formal assessment completed, what type of information can parents provide?

### Important data from parents

- *Cues or prompts*: Think of all the ways you remind your child what to do, how to do it, or when to do it. If you were gone overnight or for a weekend, would your child realize what needed to be done or would he depend on you to remind him?

- *Living away from home*: If your teen has never been away from home without you and she would like to live away from home after high school, it's important for her to experience living away while in high school. School trips, travel, retreats, or summer programs or camps are possibilities. Experiencing time away from home provides helpful information to guide your child's preparation for extended time away. You do not want your teen's first experience living away to be when he goes to college.

- *Practicing staying alone*: If you and your teen are comfortable with the idea, he can stay alone at home while you are away overnight. Have local adults as backups in case there is an emergency or a safety question.

- *Running errands*: Can your teen shop for her personal care items? Can she ask store clerks for help or information?

- *Connecting to others*: Is your teen able to reach out to friends or acquaintances? What forms of communication is he able to use? Does he know how to use social media safely?

- *Problem solving*: When your teen is faced with dilemmas, is she able to think through the problem and try to resolve it? When faced with challenges does she retreat and ignore them or ask for help?

- *Perspective taking*: Does your teen recognize other points of view as valid, even if not his own? Is he able to recognize the difference between facts and opinions?

- *Being flexible*: Is your teen able to manage a change in her routine? Can she handle changes imposed by teachers, coaches, or group leaders? Can your teen understand and cope with shifting priorities?

## How to help our children solve problems

Let's return to our parent topic night on raising capable kids and hear from Bob, dad of 8-year-old Eddie. "Getting out the door in the morning is horrible," Bob began. "Eddie's such a sweet kid, but he always seems distracted and gets lost in thought. Yesterday started out promising, but it fell apart like it does every other morning."

"Eddie, get dressed and come have breakfast," Bob said as Eddie was putting together a giant jigsaw puzzle of insects. "We need to leave a little early for school because I have an appointment."

"Ten minutes later Eddie still wasn't at the table," Bob lamented. "I went back to his room and he was on the floor, just where I left him, still working on his puzzle."

"Eddie, c'mon, you need to get dressed and eat breakfast," Bob explained in a tight voice. "We need to leave the house soon." Bob felt his breathing getting fast and shallow. He didn't want another morning where he ended up yelling until they were out the door and on their way to school.

"In a minute," Eddie finally responded. "I'm almost done with this part. I just need to finish."

"No Eddie. Get dressed now. Change out of your pajamas. Put your clothes on. Come eat breakfast. Brush your teeth. Put your lunch in your backpack. Let's go," Bob demanded through clenched teeth.

"You have to help me," Eddie squealed. "I can't do it all. I'm gonna be late!"

"Eddie, you can get dressed by yourself," Bob said. "I have to finish getting ready too. You get dressed and then we can eat breakfast together quickly before we have to leave."

Bob went back to Eddie's room five minutes later. Eddie was staring at his clothes and playing with the puzzle pieces. "Eddie, you need to get dressed right now!" Bob said as he pulled Eddie out of his clothes while muttering under his breath.

"I don't know where things went so wrong," Bob wondered. "Eddie can dress himself and he knows how to brush his teeth and put his lunch in his bag. But if I didn't help him, he wouldn't be ready when we had to leave. How do I get him to do what he needs to do when he needs to do it?"

Getting children out of the house in the morning is a common problem. It can be frustrating to watch children falter with a task they've been able to do independently. So what do we say or do when they are stuck, without doing the work for them?

### Using declarative language to encourage problem solving

Sarah Ward, a speech and language pathologist specializing in executive functioning challenges, suggests using declarative language—stating what you know or think in the form of a comment—to promote the development of problem solving. Adults often use imperative language with children—either asking a question that has a right and wrong answer or telling children what to do. But imperative language doesn't help our children think through what they need to do or say. On the other hand, declarative language encourages our children to generate their own "I" statements ("I need to organize my binder—it's gotten too messy"), and promotes the development of their inner voice (Sweeney 2010). So how can we build this way of talking into our conversations with our children, instead of telling them exactly what they need to do?

Ward offers the following examples of how we can use declarative language with our kids. We can say:

- *I wonder*: Instead of rushing in to tell children what to do or getting exasperated because you know they have handled this problem on their own before, ask the following:

  - "I wonder what you might try?"

  - "I wonder what has worked for you in the past?"

  - "I wonder why this might be happening and what might help?"

- *Hmm…that does sound challenging, I wonder*: Acknowledging the difficult situation while staying calm keeps the interaction neutral. You are helping your child slow down and think it through.

- *Zoom out*: When our children get too focused on details, they have a hard time seeing the big picture. Reminding them to "zoom out" helps them to scan for relevant information in their environment.

- *I see*: This can be used to point out relevant cues your child may be missing. It changes the conversations from you telling your child what to do toward you pointing out information to help them formulate what *they* need to do. Try saying the following:

  - "I see clothes on the floor," instead of, "Pick up your clothes."

- "I see papers are falling out of your backpack," instead of, "Put your papers in your binder."

- "I see that our friends are getting ready to leave," instead of, "Say goodbye to your friend."

## Building resilience

Let's return to our parent topic night on raising capable kids and hear what Jackie, mom of 6-year-old Jessie, had to say.

"Jessie is a perfectionist. If he's doing a drawing or building a Lego creation he can't stop until the picture or model matches the idea in his head. It rarely does and he gets so mad at himself. He'll tell me that he's so stupid. We don't expect him to be perfect, but he expects it from himself. If he makes a mistake, he doesn't shrug it off, instead it seems to paralyze him. He won't think about how to change to address the mistake, he'll just give up or destroy what he's working on or have a meltdown. How do we help him to go with the flow?"

Jessie is having a hard time managing his own expectations and emotional reactions. He isn't aware that becoming proficient with a new activity takes a combination of instruction, practice, reflection, and feedback. Many children with Asperger's don't realize this process exists because some abilities come easily for them. It can be a shock to their systems when they bump up against a task or subject that requires them to expend concerted effort to learn it. It often makes them feel as if they have failed.

Sometimes our children feel incompetent because the match between the task and their abilities is poorly coordinated. Sometimes it is because the environment does not feel safe. Teachers, coaches, or peers may bully our children as they struggle with a concept or behavior that classmates have already mastered. Parents or other adults may show exasperation or frustration when expectations aren't met. We need to provide just enough of a challenge to stretch our child's abilities in a safe environment. Too much challenge and our children feel they are failures. Too little and they assume we don't believe they are capable of much.

## *Helping our children become more resilient*

- *Normalize mistakes*: Think out loud about the mistakes you make while learning something new or challenging. Let your child know that everyone, no matter how old or experienced, makes mistakes. Clarify that making mistakes is part of the learning process. Be a role model and stay calm when glitches occur.

- *Focus on abilities and interests*: Make sure your child has time to explore interests and use skills. It's easier for your child to recover from missteps when he feels appreciated for his strengths and has time to relax and enjoy current interests.

- *Practice solving problems*: Provide opportunities to think through problems and practice resolving them. Help your child shift from feeling overwhelmed by a complication to analyzing how to address it. Sometimes, using visual problem solving charts can help your child imagine possible solutions.

## *Creating Asperger's / autism-spectrum-friendly environments*

We cannot expect our children to learn and practice the skills they need if the environments they find themselves in are inhospitable to someone with AS or on the autism spectrum. Just as we would struggle in an environment that caused us tremendous stress, our children cannot demonstrate their proficiencies when their surroundings are unreceptive. We need to think about how to create and advocate for AS-friendly environments.

I was recently talking with my cousin, Max Veggeberg, the CEO at Homeworks Energy, Inc. He had called because he had hired a few adults with Asperger's and wanted to make sure his company was creating a supportive work environment for his new employees. As he explained the jobs he asked, "What else can I do to help them succeed at work?" I wanted to jump through the phone and hug him because that is exactly the type of question we all need to be asking.

"I'd recommend putting any expectations or directions in writing and having an employee manual that explains any policies or procedures you expect them to follow," I suggested.

"What about personal space?" Max asked. "Do I need to make sure that people aren't too close together?"

"That depends on the person," I answered. "I think you can ask if they are comfortable with sharing a work space or if they need a bit more privacy. Often, people with Asperger's have sensory sensitivities. They might have a hard time with certain sounds that they can't ignore, or the light might feel too intense, or there might be smells that make them uncomfortable. If any of your new employees seem sensitive in these areas, you can easily provide accommodations like earbuds or noise cancelling headphones or changing light fixtures."

Veggeberg sets a wonderful example for what you hope your child or adult will encounter when they venture into new environments. He is doing all he can to bring out the best in his employees by providing an accommodating environment. When I asked if he had any other questions or whether what we had discussed made sense, he said, "It's just common sense, Brenda." Now if Veggeberg could encourage other business owners to follow his lead, we'd be all set!

I've also gotten calls from teachers, clinicians, and parents who want to ensure that the children in their care are provided with environments that are conducive to learning and participating at school, home or out in the community.

WHAT SHOULD WE CONSIDER WHEN WE TRY
TO CREATE AS-FRIENDLY SETTINGS?

- *Build positive relationships*: My son always knew when a teacher didn't like him. And he was able to establish positive relationships with many teachers who understood his profile of strengths and challenges and worked with him to help him succeed. If the teacher or adult in charge doesn't understand Asperger's and views your child's behavior as intentional, it will be hard for your child to thrive in that environment. We need to provide helpful and practical information to adults who work with our children, so that they can be effective and support successful inclusion.

- *Develop routines*: There are a multitude of tasks we expect our children to master, but our children have a difficult time categorizing and organizing the various components within each task. If we develop routines, we help them see how all the individual pieces fit together to complete the job. We can create routines with our children so that they learn how to complete them on a regular basis. Sarah Ward suggests taking a picture of the end result (a dressed child or a backpack ready for school) and then asking your child to "match the picture." You can also ask your child to help you create a list to clarify the steps involved in any given routine, such as the following examples.

  ○ Morning routine: I need to get dressed, wash my face and brush my teeth, eat breakfast, and put my lunch in my backpack.

  ○ Evening routine: I need to make sure I have all my work in my backpack, take a shower, and read in bed.

  ○ Cleaning room routine: I need to put the dirty clothes in the laundry basket, put the clean clothes in my dresser, throw away any garbage, recycle papers or bottles, put books on bookshelves, and put toys in cubbies.

- *Recognize capabilities*: All children with AS have strengths; make sure parents and teachers recognize and utilize these strengths. The focused attention on capabilities helps our children see their merits, which is particularly important when they are so often reminded of their challenges.

- *Highlight relevant information in the environment*: Our children don't recognize which details are important and what stimuli can be ignored. Peter Vermeulen, in his book, *Autism as Context Blindness*, clarifies that we can't teach children on the autism spectrum context sensitivity, but we can teach them to compensate for their difficulty with it. He recommends that we clarify the context that children on the autism spectrum don't spontaneously intuit. This includes pointing out relevant information to pay attention to and minimizing sensory distractions (Vermeulen 2012).

- *Make the implicit explicit*: There are multiple opportunities for children with AS to misunderstand what we want them to do because of how we communicate our message. We need to make our requests and expectations explicit. We can't assume that the implied and subtle messages we give will be interpreted correctly.

- *Clarify alternative perspectives*: Often, our children get stuck in thinking that their point of view is the only correct understanding of a situation. We have to remember that they aren't being inflexible in order to make our lives more difficult. They are stuck because they might not be accurately assessing relevant contextual information that would clarify what is happening and how to respond. Our children might be relying on prior understandings or experiences, which could be unhelpful in their current situation. Vermeulen points out that we should ask, "Which context does he not see or is he unable to imagine?" (Vermeulen 2012, p.368). This refocuses our attention on what relevant information or connection our children are missing so that we can draw their attention to the meaning they missed.

- *Analyze sensory needs*: If our children have sensory sensitivities, they can feel overwhelmed and anxious in certain settings. Try to determine whether any sensory needs might be impacting their ability to function successfully in the environment. You can also consider different sensory activities that help children calm down or perk up depending on their particular needs. Some children find the following activities or accommodations useful.

- *Jumping*: Some kids enjoy trampolines. My mom made a jumping pit for my boys by sewing fleece fabric into a rectangle shape and stuffing it with foam pieces with a Velcro closure.

- *Bean box*: I filled an under-the-bed plastic sweater box with all types of dried beans and peas. I'd put all kinds of shapes and small pieces into the box and have my sons look for them.

- *Swing*: Some families use swings at the playground or an indoor hammock swing.

- *Body Sox®*: Search on the web for Body Sox if your kids like having deep pressure against their body.

- *Cooking*: Kneading dough and mixing can be a nice activity for kids to get sensory input and build strength.

- *Playing with Play-Doh or Lego, writing*: All these types of activities can help your child increase their fine motor capabilities while having fun (if they like these types of activities). Remember, there is always more than one way to help your child with sensory sensitivities. If one activity isn't a good fit, it may be worth trying a different approach.

- *Identify potential triggers*: Our kids need to understand what situations are frustrating or anxiety producing for them. It also helps to know what activities bring a sense of calm and relaxation. I've used *The Incredible 5-Point Scale* by Buron and Curtis (2003), *Social Behavior and Self-Management: 5-Point Scales for Adolescents and Adults* by Buron et al. (2012), *My Book Full of Feelings* by Jaffe and

Gardner (2006), and *Exploring Feelings: Cognitive Behaviour Therapy to Manage Anxiety* by Attwood (2004) to help my children explore their triggers, anxiety, and emotions. It helped us understand what situations made things worse and what we could do to lower their stress.

- *Develop a calming toolbox*: Our children need to learn how to lower their anxiety. Help them figure out which activities make them feel calmer. See specific suggestions in Chapter 3.

- *Raise awareness*: When you are able, it's very helpful to join a group that raises awareness of issues of concern to children and adults with Asperger's and works to minimize challenges and foster opportunities. Some parents do this through special education parent groups connected to their schools. Some join organizations, like AANE, that do legislative advocacy and provide training and consultation for professionals and parents.

## Setting panic aside

It is hard to know when to push and when to let a child be. What we hope is that our children's ability to be interdependent and independent will improve as they practice using these skills at home, in school, and out in the community. And we hope that they are exposed to environments that provide the right amount of support and challenge. We can't be certain about the length of time required for our kids to become adept in the areas that are difficult for them. We can provide unconditional love and acceptance as they practice and become more familiar with challenging or confusing life skills.

# Conclusion

*Setting Panic Aside*

When we moved from New Jersey to Massachusetts in 2005 I had a lot on my mind. I was worried that Noah wouldn't adjust to his new school. I was concerned that his classmates wouldn't reach out to him and he wouldn't find a friend. I felt unsure about what Daniel needed—he was either incredibly impulsive or in dire need of comfort. And Josh wasn't talking and didn't seem at all frustrated with his inability to communicate with us.

I spent those first few months getting my children settled. Even though certain situations worked out for the boys (Noah had a wonderful teacher and made a friend and Daniel's class was the right fit), it was hard to enjoy these moments because I still felt overwhelmed. I knew in the long run this move was good for us all, but it was hard to believe it in the beginning.

A few months after moving, I attended an AANE parent support group. One of the first questions Jean Stern, Director of Children's Services, asked was, "What do you do to take care of yourself?" I looked at Jean and started to cry. "Nothing," I replied, "I don't do anything to take care of myself." With that one question, Jean put me on the path to help me reclaim what had been lost—perspective and resilience.

The move to Massachusetts had churned up a lot of anxiety for me. Fear of the unknown had run rampant as I worried about providing my kids what they needed. I was concerned that I might miss an opportunity that would alter their developmental course for the better. It took breaking down in the support group for me to realize that my panic had taken control. I thank Jean every day for asking the right question at the right time.

We all worry about our children at times. Not every moment is great (and some are really tough), but many moments are wonderful. Parents want to know if their children will be okay. They want to know what the future holds. I am full of hope for my own children and yours too. I hope that we are laying the foundation for them to understand themselves and the world around them. I hope that they believe in themselves and appreciate their abilities. I hope that the challenges and problems they encounter build their sense of resilience and bravery. And I hope they know how glad we are to have them in our lives.

Our children need our understanding, acceptance, love, and guidance. When you start to feel anxious about the unknown, a problem you can't seem to resolve, or someone else's reaction to your child, think about the stories throughout the book that were meaningful to you and remember that you are not alone. Use the suggestions to approach on-going dilemmas in a new way. Remember that you can set your worries down for a moment and do something with your child that you both enjoy. I hope this book has asked you the right question at the right time and that you find more balance and joy to parent with less panic.

# References

Attwood, T. (2004) *Exploring Feelings: Cognitive Behaviour Therapy To Manage Anxiety*. Arlington, TX: Future Horizons Inc.

Attwood, T. (2007) *The Complete Guide to Asperger's Syndrome*. London and Philadelphia, PA: Jessica Kingsley Publishers.

Buron, K. (2006) *When My Worries Get Too Big! A Relaxation Book for children Who Live With Anxiety*. Shawnee Mission, KS: Autism Asperger Publishing Company.

Buron, K. (2012) *Adalyn Clare*. Shawnee Mission, KS: Autism Asperger Publishing Company.

Buron, K. and Curtis, M. (2003) *The Incredible 5-Point Scale*. Shawnee Mission, KS: Autism Asperger Publishing Company.

Buron, K., Brown, J., Curtis, M. and King, L. (2012) *Social Behavior and Self-Management: 5-Point Scales for Adolescents and Adults*. Shawnee Mission, KS: Autism Asperger Publishing Company.

Coulter, D. (2007) *Understanding Brothers and Sisters on the Autism Spectrum*. Winston-Salem, NC: Coulter Video Publishing.

Dater, B. (2008) *Asperger Syndrome/ASD: The Big Picture*. Watertown, MA: Asperger's Association of New England (AANE).

Dawson, P. and Guare, R. (2009) *Smart but Scattered*. New York: Guilford Press.

Drezner, E. (2012) "Throw Away the Yardstick or The Blessing of the Diagnosis." *AANE Journal, Spring* 10, 12–13.

Frender, S. and Schiffmiller, R. (2007) *Brotherly Feelings: Me, My Emotions, and my Brother with Asperger Syndrome*. London and Philadelphia. PA: Jessica Kingsley Publishers.

Gray, C. (2010) *The New Social Story™ Book*. Arlington, TX: Future Horizons.

Howlin, R. (2003) *Asperger Syndrome: Social Dyslexia*. Kalamazoo, MI: Asperger Society of Michigan. Available at www.michiganallianceforfamilies.org/inf/docs/asp.social.pdf, accessed on 8 December 2013.

Huebner, D. (2006) *What to Do When You Worry Too Much: A Kid's Guide to Overcoming Anxiety*. Washington, DC: Magination Press.

Huebner, D. (2008) *What to Do When Your Temper Flares: A Kid's Guide to Overcoming Problems with Anger*. Washington, DC: Magination Press.

Jaffe, A. and Gardner, L. (2006) *My Book Full of Feelings*. Shawnee Mission, KS: Autism Asperger Publishing Company.

Korin, E. (2006) *Asperger Syndrome: An Owner's Manual: What You, Your Parents and Your Teachers Need to Know*. Shawnee Mission, KS: Autism Asperger Publishing Company.

Korin, E. (2007) *Asperger Syndrome: An Owner's Manual 2 For Older Adolescents and Adults: What You, Your Parents and Friends, and Your Employer, Need to Know*. Shawnee Mission, KS: Autism Asperger Publishing Company.

Lavoie, R. (2005) *Social Skill Autopsies: A Strategy to Promote and Develop Social Competencies*. Arlington, VA: LDonline. Available at www.ldonline.org/article/14910, accessed on 8 December 2013.

Myles, B. and Southwick, J. (2005) *Asperger Syndrome and Difficult Moments: Practical Solutions for Tantrums, Rage, and Meltdowns*. Shawnee Mission, KS: Autism Asperger Publishing Company.

Myles, B., Schelvan, R. and Trautman, M. (2004) *The Hidden Curriculum: Practical Solutions for Understanding Unstated Rules in Social Situations*. Shawnee Mission, KS: Autism Asperger Publishing Company.

Page, T. (2009) *Parallel Play: Growing up with Undiagnosed Asperger's*. New York and Toronto: Doubleday.

Rubin, E. (2013) *Thinking About Siblings*. Zeh Lezeh blog. Available at www.zehlezeh.wordpress.com/2013/04/11/thinking-about-siblings, accessed on 8 December 2013.

Sweeney, D. (2010) *Thinking About the Language We Use with Children with ASD*. ReConnect Autism blog. Available at http://reconnectautism.blogspot.com/2010/05/thinking-about-language-we-use-with.html, accessed on 8 December 2013.

Vermeulen, P. (2012) *Autism As Context Blindness*. Shawnee Mission, KS: Autism Asperger Publishing Company.

Winner, M. (2000) *Inside Out What Makes A Person With Social Cognitive Deficits Tick?* San Jose, CA: Social Thinking.

Winner, M. (2007) *Social Behavior Mapping*. San Jose, CA: Social Thinking.

# *Additional Resources*

For current book and video recommendations, please visit the following websites:

- www.aane.org
- www.jkp.com

## Helpful websites

There are many websites available—but not all are created equal! These are some of my favorites:

- Asperger's Association of New England (AANE)

  www.aane.org

- Sarah Ward's website

  www.cognitiveconnectionstherapy.com

- Kari Dunn Buron's website

  www.5pointscale.com

- Tony Attwood's website

  www.tonyattwood.com.au

- Michelle Garcia Winner's website

  www.socialthinking.com

# *Index*